My Year of Practicing

POSITIVE PSYCHOLOGY

50 Fabulous Feats @ 50

SUSAN M. MIFSUD

BALBOA.
PRESS
A DIVISION OF HAY HOUSE

Copyright © 2018 Susan M. Mifsud.

All rights reserved. No part of this book may be used or reproduced by any means, graphic, electronic, or mechanical, including photocopying, recording, taping or by any information storage retrieval system without the written permission of the author except in the case of brief quotations embodied in critical articles and reviews.

This book is a work of non-fiction. Unless otherwise noted, the author and the publisher make no explicit guarantees as to the accuracy of the information contained in this book and in some cases, names of people and places have been altered to protect their privacy.

Balboa Press books may be ordered through booksellers or by contacting:

Balboa Press
A Division of Hay House
1663 Liberty Drive
Bloomington, IN 47403
www.balboapress.com
1 (877) 407-4847

Because of the dynamic nature of the Internet, any web addresses or links contained in this book may have changed since publication and may no longer be valid. The views expressed in this work are solely those of the author and do not necessarily reflect the views of the publisher, and the publisher hereby disclaims any responsibility for them.

The author of this book does not dispense medical advice or prescribe the use of any technique as a form of treatment for physical, emotional, or medical problems without the advice of a physician, either directly or indirectly. The intent of the author is only to offer information of a general nature to help you in your quest for emotional and spiritual well-being. In the event you use any of the information in this book for yourself, which is your constitutional right, the author and the publisher assume no responsibility for your actions.

Any people depicted in stock imagery provided by Getty Images are models, and such images are being used for illustrative purposes only. Certain stock imagery © Getty Images.

Print information available on the last page.

ISBN: 978-1-9822-0410-5 (sc)
ISBN: 978-1-9822-0411-2 (e)

Balboa Press rev. date: 05/17/2018

Contents

Introduction ix

Practicing Gratitude 1

Cultivating Optimism 21

Practicing Acts Of Kindness 39

Nurturing Social Relationships 59

Developing Coping Strategies 91

Savouring Life's Joys 125

Committing To Your Goals 143

Taking Care Of Your Body – Exercise................. 177

Taking Care Of Your Mind – Mindfulness..........191

Taking Care Of Your Soul – Spirituality 205

References... 231

To my beautiful boys,
Christian and Michael.
You are, and will always be,
my most Fabulous Feats.

Introduction

I have always loved writing. I still have the yellowing crumpled pages of a book I began when I was in the third grade; it was about a mischievous bunny and I had written the first four chapters. Unfortunately, I also can see the many erasure marks on the pages signaling my continuous editing that, even then, snatched away my joy and replaced it with anxiety and doubt – chapter five was never written.

While I wasn't aware at the time, this pattern was an early example of the excessive 'nervousness' that punctuated my life. Anxiety and depression accompanied me on my life's journey, not that I had any intention of admitting this for many years, especially to myself. It was in my thirties when I came to terms with the fact that I lived with mental illness.

Since that time, I have accepted that the illness is part of me, but doesn't define me. As an individual with a good job and a privileged life, I felt it was incumbent on me to share my story with others, putting a face to mental illness. In 2008 I began speaking with the Canadian Mental Health Association – Niagara Branch about my experiences.

Similarly, I wanted the message to be one infused with hope of recovery. I investigated mental illness and the ways in which an individual can positively impact their own wellbeing, whether living with mental illness or not. A series of life events pointed me down a road that I could not have anticipated, beginning with being hired as a volunteer Mental Health Blogger with Healthy Minds Canada.

My love of writing was combined with my passion for stigma reduction, and I started to share my stories, thoughts, and ideas with a broader audience.

Interestingly, the very nature of blogging assisted me with my anxiety related to my writing abilities. When you need to produce a post ever couple of weeks, while maintaining a full life of work and volunteering, you cannot spend endless hours on revising your materials; blogging allowed me to say it, edit it once or twice, and release it to the world.

A year later, I found myself ushering in a series of major life changes: the loss of the job I had worked at for more than 26 years; the subsequent decision to take the opportunity to return to school to complete my Master's degree with an emphasis on applied positive psychology and mental health; the launching of my own blog site; the creation of my own consulting company; and a career change that saw me providing direct support to individuals living with severe and persistent mental illness. Whew!

This book represents the realization of a dream that the little girl writing about a naughty rabbit all those years ago would have celebrated. I hope that I am able to inspire others to embrace 'the upside of life's transformations' by choosing to engage in your own Fabulous Feats towards a life of practicing gratitude, cultivating optimism, practicing acts of kindness, nurturing social relationships, developing coping strategies, savouring life's joys, committing to your goals and taking care of your mind, body, and spirit.

Wishing you wellness, Susan Mifsud
#FabFeats

January 14, 2018

WELCOME TO SILVERLININGFROG

The creation of SilverLiningFrog represents the fulfilment of a dream for me. Having had the privilege to be a Mental Health Blogger with Healthy Minds Canada for the last year, I have come to love being able to share my thoughts, ideas, and understanding related to mental illness from the perspective of someone with lived experience.

In my first post, I wanted to provide a little background regarding the origins of my site name. I have closely identified with the frog as my symbol for many years; my favourite Muppet is, of course, Kermit, and, over time, as people came to know my interest in frogs, the number of stuffed animals, pictures, and figures I received filled my home and office. But, over the years, I experienced my share of life challenges and the frog became more than just something to collect; it came to be my animal spirit. The frog represents metamorphosis; it supports clarity and the ability to accept the changes that come with life transformations – the good and the bad. On my 46th birthday, I had a frog tattooed on my ankle (I have told my young adult sons that they, too, can get tattoos on their 46th birthdays) to remind me that life is all about growth and change.

The "silver lining" comes from my choice in seeing opportunity in the wake of most challenges. While my issues with depression and anxiety have been debilitating at various points in my life, living with mental illness has also allowed me to examine my life and my priorities and I believe I know myself better as a result. And, although I don't believe that things happen for a reason – there are too many terrible things that happen for me to understand the world in this way – I do think you can create meaning and purpose from difficult situations. According to Sonja Lyubomirsky in *The Myths of Happiness*, the greatest adaptive strategy for traumatic situations involves dissecting and systematically analyzing painful times to better understand them, gain some meaning from them, and thereby, get past them.

I hope that through SilverLiningFrog I will be able to continue my life's journey by sharing my passion for mental health education, advocacy, and stigma elimination. Thank you for those who choose to join me in the next stage of my adventure.

February 8, 2015

50 FABULOUS FEATS @ 50

Next month marks my half century year. While some women avoid admitting to such milestone, I have decided to embrace my 50th year wholeheartedly. This year-long adventure I am calling 50 Fabulous Feats @ 50, in which I will prove that you can teach a middle-aged dog new tricks by engaging in a series of "firsts" for me.

Each week I will pick something that is new to me and expand my world just a little by meeting, visiting, or doing something that I've never done before. I plan to blog about my experiences, thoughts, and learnings. Before you get too excited, however, you need to understand a couple of things about me. I have spent much of my life as a scaredy cat: I live with anxiety, and have lived a rather safe, risk-averse life. As a result, some of my firsts may be laughable to "normal" folks. I have never ridden on a motorcycle, gone horseback riding, or eaten escargot. I also want to explore both my inner and outer worlds so one week I may go up in a hot air balloon, while the next I could go on a spiritual retreat. Finally, I want to give back to the world that has given me so much love, support, and beauty; I plan to engage in activities with meaning and purpose to express my gratitude for all the prosperity in my life through such things as donating blood, planting trees, and working for charitable causes. While these "feats" may seem mundane to some, they will be "fabulous" to me.

I hope you will join me on my journey vicariously and, perhaps, in person if you think you might like to participate in a feat that resonates with you too. I'm excited about my year of firsts and can't wait to hit the big 5-0 to start!

June 24, 2015

MY POSITIVE PSYCHOLOGY EXPERIMENT

In my last blog I introduced my intention to pursue a year-long adventure quest that I am calling 50 Fabulous Feats @ 50. My impetus for the project is multi-faceted, but a key reason is to engage in my own positive psychology experiment. I have lived with depression and anxiety for my entire adult life. For me, medication supports my ongoing mental health, but it has been important for me to explore those things within my control that can enhance my well-being. I have spent time reading about the latest research, particularly around positive psychology.

While I am hardly able to do justice to the work done in this field in this brief blog, my experiment was inspired by Sonja Lyubomirsky's research which suggests "dynamic, episodic, novel, and attention-enticing" intentional activities support increased and lasting well-being (see http://sonjalyubomirsky. com/). So, my plan to do 50 things that I have never done before is about deliberately enhancing my own happiness.

It has been great fun over the last couple of weeks to share my ideas for the 50 Feats @ 50 adventure with family, friends, and strangers alike, asking for opinions and suggestions about what I should add to the list. Such interesting and wildly different answers: the CN Tower EdgeWalk is a popular one; skydiving is another that has come up frequently.

I must note that I am both scared of heights and rather risk averse, so, while these might be just right for some folks, neither made it on to my list. Others had more sentimental suggestions: send a message in a bottle out to sea; go on a romantic picnic. I like these, so they might make the cut. Still others offered not only their recommendations, but to join me in the pursuits: horseback riding, hot air ballooning, canoeing, afternoon tea at an elegant establishment, bird watching. They all sound like great fun, made better by the added bonus of having friends to share the experiences. Still others came up with things I would never have thought of myself: going to a shooting range, attending a dog show (I am assured it is just like the movie Best in Show), going to a fortune teller to find out what the next 50 years have in store for me. I have also added the feats that involve giving back to my community: planting a tree (or 50 of them) for posterity, donating blood, serving at a homeless shelter. Then, there are the personal health and wellness feats: running (or walking really fast) in a 5 K race; maintaining a meditation practice; taking a yoga class. Finally, there are a few feats that are particularly special to me. People who know me well (okay, even in passing) are aware that Kermit the Frog is my hero. I grew up with Sesame Street and The Muppet Show, and love all the movies (1999's Muppets From Space does not count). Like most people, I want to meet my hero, but only recently figured out how I could do this. Kermit, as well as a number of his Muppet companions, can be found at the National Museum of American History in Washington, D.C. Sounds like a road trip could be in the cards for me!

So, T minus two weeks to the launch of 50 feats. For anyone with more ideas to share, I'd love to hear them; and if you want to participate in a fabulous feat or two, please drop me a line. What's better than 50 Fabulous Feats @ 50? Easy: 50 Fabulous Feats @50 with Friends!

July 6, 2015

PILLAR OF POSITIVITY #1:
Practicing Gratitude

Even though I love the holiday season, I experience stress during the hustle and bustle that accompanies this time of year and I know I am not alone in getting a bit tense and anxious. The first #FabFeats "pillar of positivity" I have chosen, therefore, is the **practice of gratitude.**

Robert Emmons defines gratitude as "a felt sense of wonder, thankfulness, and appreciation for life." Brene Brown (brenebrown.com), who has conducted extensive research on gratitude, has discovered that a commonality among people who are living joyful lives is their inclusion of gratitude in their daily activities. While our Neanderthal ancestors needed to be attuned to threats to survive, unfortunately, even though we no longer regularly battle wild animals for survival, our brains are still wired towards a negative focus. The practice of gratitude reconnects us to an awareness of the positives in life.

The benefits of practicing gratitude are numerous: less depression, anxiety, envy; better able to cope with stress; increased social bonds; more energy, hopeful; more frequent positive emotions; higher self-esteem.

I have experimented with a number of gratitude techniques in order to find those that resonate particularly with me. Below are a few exercises and suggestions that you may wish to try:

- **Keeping a gratitude journal:** There are many variations on the gratitude journal. Research suggests that writing once or twice a week rather than daily is most effective. Keep an ongoing list of people for whom you are thankful and why. Going into detail can be more beneficial than making a longer, but more superficial, list. In the end, do what feels comfortable for you and put some time aside so that you are present and aware when you are recording in your journal.
- **Write a Gratitude Letter:** Take a few minutes to write a letter to someone expressing thanks for what they have contributed to your life. Be specific. If possible, personally deliver the letter and read it aloud to the person. Not only will you benefit, so will the receiver.
- **Fill a Gratitude Box:** Decorate a box and place items that remind you of a happy memory (concert ticket stub, thank you note, picture, etc.) in it. Every week, spend a few minutes looking through and reliving experiences.
- **Create a Gratitude Board:** Create a collage of things for which you are grateful and place it in a spot that you will regularly see

it. Change up the items from time to time to keep it fresh.

- **Throw a Gratitude Party:** Invite some friends over and ask them each to write a short note about something for which they are grateful. Read aloud or share the notes with each other.

It's time to start the movement – Join me and we will infuse our holiday celebrations with gratitude.

I don't have to chase extraordinary moments to find happiness – it's right in front of me if I'm paying attention and practicing gratitude. -Brene Brown

December 10, 2015

#FABFEATS: 100 WOMEN WHO CARE – NIAGARA

One of the main goals for my 50 Feats was to find ways of giving back to my community. A little searching took me to the website for 100 Women Who Care – Niagara. The organization is worldwide with 350 chapters in the U.S., Canada, Mexico, Singapore, the Caribbean, and British Isles. Niagara's group is organized by Sylvia Berezowski and has a membership of over 170 women. The idea behind 100 Women is to provide funds to local community causes by coming together for an hour at 4 times during the year and donating $100 per person on these occasions to a selected Niagara charity. In a single hour, 3 charities that have been nominated by members are randomly selected and their representatives provide a brief explanation of the cause and how monies will be used if chosen. Members then vote and one of the charities wins the donations for that meeting.

This wonderful group is completely volunteer-run, resulting in all the money collected going directly to the organizations selected. An amazing $17,000 -$19,000 has been donated to each of the chosen organizations in the last 2 years. I am especially appreciative of also having the opportunity not only to support my community, but also learn about a number of not-for-profits and charities that I didn't even know existed in Niagara including support for children's breakfast programs, mentorships, hospice, native women, and supportive cancer care.

The meeting I attended saw a room full of dedicated women in attendance, despite them having to brave a particularly cold evening. The evening began with a presentation from the last meeting's recipient: Big Brothers and Big Sisters of Niagara Falls. The Executive Director spoke eloquently about their individual and group mentoring programs for children and the positive impact that the $17,100 donated by 100 Women will provide.

Next, the evening's 3 charities were randomly selected from the 25 that had been nominated by members. Representatives for The Learning Disabilities Association of Niagara, TASC Niagara (supporting children and adults living with disabilities), and The David Gregory Mckinnon Memorial Foundation (education and advocacy for families affected by kidney disease) each gave heartfelt presentations about their charities.

I found it difficult to choose from these wonderful organizations, but am comforted by the fact that those who are not selected are eligible to be considered again. As well, knowing that the funds donated will go to a great cause no matter who wins makes it very easy to give.

As my sister is a kidney donation recipient (her husband gave her one of his kidneys – talk about true love!), I have a special place in my heart for lifesaving organ transplant programs. In addition, the presentation by David's mother about the loss of her beautiful son, and her mission to raise funds to support others living with kidney disease in his name, was powerful, especially to a room full of Moms like me. David's charity was selected.

We wrote our cheques out to the Foundation, and the whole event was wrapped up in one hour. I feel privileged to participate in this group with incredible, caring women, giving back, pooling our resources to support our local community. For only 4 hours and $400 over the course of a year, 100 Women Who Care Niagara is proof positive that one person can make a difference, and when they come together, 100+ women can change our world.

More information about joining 100 Women Who Care in your area can be found at http://www.100womenwhocare.org/.

February 16, 2016

#FABFEATS: WOMEN & WELLNESS NIAGARA

The original Women & Wellness (W & W) event began in Moncton, New Brunswick in 2004 when Helen MacDonnell hosted a "kitchen party with a purpose" in order to raise awareness and decrease the stigma associated with mental illness after the death of her brother by suicide. She invited 54 friends and family to her home and raised $1,200 for the Moncton branch of the Canadian Mental Health Association.

Since that time, W & W has raised over $500,000 in donations for CMHAs from events across Canada. I have been privileged to be involved with the Women & Wellness Niagara organizing committee since its inception in 2011. At that time, I was one of 7 volunteers, inspired by our fearless and dynamic leader, Elaine Edmiston. That year, we invited 3 local women from the CMHA Speakers' Bureau to share their stories and welcomed just over 100 guest who enjoyed a glass of wine, some appetizers and the companionship of like-minded, caring women.

Each year we learned a little more, and grew accordingly. We welcomed other amazing keynote and wellness speakers who presented their own stories and challenges – Karen Liberman, Jan Wong, Rona Maynard, Alicia Raimundo. We expanded our committee members and increased sponsorships. We added a raffle and door prizes into the mix, migrated registration to Eventbrite.

And every event attracted more women than the year before; by our 5th year we had more than 500 women attending.

This year, Women and Wellness morphed again. We changed our venue to Club Roma in St. Catharines to accommodate more than 650 women. We selected Valerie Pringle as our keynote speaker. In addition to the raffle, we put together a silent auction and penny sale for the night of the event. Most exciting for me, we commissioned a performance from a local theatre group, Something Something Productions, which they wrote especially for us.

After months of planning, the day of the event was upon us. Thanks to our Chairperson, Karla Gilmore, all the details were covered. The penny sale and silent auction items were set up in the foyer, and more than 50 volunteers assumed their roles as ushers, ticket sellers, guides, greeters, and counters. If you build it, they do come, beginning with a trickle of early birds at 5:45 and rising to a tsunami just after 6:00. The buzz in the lobby foretold the success of the evening. When doors to the main room opened, the women (and a few brave men) were escorted to their seats. Each table was decorated with green napkins representing mental health and a beautiful flower arrangement from Vermeers. In addition to wine available at the bar, cider, hot appetizers, and an assortment of desserts were set out on the tables.

Our speaker, Valerie Pringle, arrived with a smile and lovely down-to-earth manner, telling us that she knew how complicated these kinds of events were and that she was fine to look after herself while we managed the crowds and last-minute details. Fortunately, other than a little glitch with the video and audio equipment, the evening progressed smoothly.

At 6:30, our wonderful MC for the evening, Ruth Unrau, began to call everyone to their seats, no small task with more than 650 attendees. As we began the program, the energy in the room was electric. Sponsors brought their greetings and our CMHA – Niagara President, Stuart Dorricott, one of a handful of men there, talked about his experiences trying to find assistance for a loved one dealing with a mental health crisis and the great importance of the event's fundraising recipient, CMHA's walk-in counselling service.

Next up, the local theatre group, Something Something Productions, performed their 3 women show. This production was the brainchild of Dina Mavridis, co-founder of the group, with her partner Rob Burke. Best known for their amazing productions of The Rocky Horrors Show LIVE upstairs at Corks in Niagara-On-The-Lake, the company is also devoted to supporting the Niagara community by raising over $6,000 for local charities. When approached about performing at our W & W event, Dina went above and beyond expectations by reaching out to the women in Niagara, asking them to share their personal stories of mental illness from which she created the monologues that came to our stage. Dina, along with 2 other exceptional female performers, brought this collaborative piece to life: stories of bi-polar disorder, post-partum depression, abuse and post-traumatic stress disorder; the shame resulting from the stigma of mental illness, the pain that makes living feel intolerable; and, most important, the hope of support, help, and recovery. There were few dry eyes at the end of their delivery as we all connected at the heart, thinking about our own struggles and those of our friends and family members.

The break that followed allowed individuals time to chat, donate, bid on the silent auction, and buy tickets for our penny sale and raffle. I was able to catch up with my friends in the audience before returning to my seat for the main attraction: Valerie Pringle. True to her broadcaster roots, Valerie's delivery was flawless – easy and conversational. She spoke of her involvement with CAMH after her husband's former law partner, Michael Wilson, lost his son to suicide. She recounted her own daughter, Catherine's struggle with panic and anxiety disorder. She described her own growth and education as a caregiver for a family member living with mental illness. She stressed hope and recovery and the importance of treatment like the walk-in counselling service. It was an honour and a pleasure to listen to her speak.

The night drew to a close with the announcement of raffle winners and the final tally of funds raised from the evening. As our Chair, Karla, approached the podium, Valerie leaned over to me with a pledge form and said she had forgotten to hand hers in to the donation desk. As we were very close to our goal for that evening of $15,000, I ran up the stairs to the stage waiving Valerie's donation. Karla casually asked if there were any more donations not yet received and to our astonishment, members of the audience began to rise and approach the stage with bundles of pledge envelopes. We had so many that we couldn't count them all before concluding the night. Suffice it to say that we exceeded our target!

In what seemed like no time at all, it was over. Our months of planning had resulted in a night we were all proud of and, though exhausted, the cleanup crew beamed with satisfaction as we packed up for another year. I am privileged to work with such exceptional women on the W & W committee. Together, we make a positive difference in our community. Even before we closed our eyes for a well-earned night's sleep, the emails were already circulating about next years' event: who we would consider for the keynote; could we increase our numbers to 1000 participants; and how else might we make next year's evening even better. Look out Niagara, W & W 2017 will knock your socks off!

[Our final tally for the evening was $18,000 in addition to pre-event sales and sponsors for an overall total of $48,000 before expenses. For our 6 years of Women and Wellness: more than 2,300 women in attendance and over $170,000 gross revenues.]

February 23, 2016

#FABFEATS: THE COLDEST NIGHT OF THE YEAR

One of the joys of engaging in my Fabulous Feats is the ability to meet wonderful people whose paths I might not have otherwise crossed. This was the case when I signed up to volunteer for The Coldest Night of the Year walk in St. Catharines.

The walk began in 2011 as a way of raising money for the hungry, homeless, and hurting across Canada. By signing up to walk 2, 5, or 10 kms, participants experience just a little of what being outside on a cold winter night is like. With an estimated 150,000 Canadians experiencing homelessness outside, and countless more facing the uncertainly of living right on the edge, the walk raises both awareness and much-needed funds in over 100 communities for people struggling with poverty, mental health and addiction issues, discrimination, homelessness, and unemployment.

In Niagara, there are a number of walks including Niagara Falls (Project Share), Welland (The Open Arms Mission of Welland), Lincoln (Community Care of West Niagara) and St. Catharines (Start Me Up Niagara). Although I live in Niagara Falls, I chose to volunteer with Start Me Up Niagara (SMUN) because I am familiar with the great work they do to support individuals living with mental illness and addictions. I went on the national website and signed up as a volunteer.

I received an email inviting me to a volunteer get together for training at SMUN. When I arrived, I met other individuals including staff members, Board Directors, and community members who were all there to help make St. Catharines' event successful. I had met Susan Venditti before, but that night I also met her partner, Tony "the Tiger" Venditti, who, in addition to being the Centre Coordinator, headed a team that had raised the 3rd largest amount compared to walkers from across Canada. I received my instructions for my role as Greeter and had a chance to get to know a few of the other volunteers over pizza.

The night of the event I arrived at the appointed time and met a lovely volunteer named Bonita who I would be working alongside. Our job was to make sure volunteers and walkers filled out the waiver form as the first step in the process. We both donned our blue event toques and began. In between giving instructions and checking paperwork, Bonita and I were able to chat. She said she was volunteering because SMUN had been so supportive for her, even helping her set up her own business. She proudly gave me a card that advertised her handmade jewelry.

It was wonderful to see the teams assemble and the little families gathered together to participate and model the importance of being a caring community member. With a few speeches, and lots of cheering, the walk began. Mother Nature was on our side, as the sun streamed into Market Square with the temperature topping out at 8 degrees. Bonita and I moved from Greeters to Welcome Back-ers. As people arrived in from their various walks, we clapped, yelled, and generally made noise that recognized the returnees.

There was food, and entertainment for everyone – general merriment and celebration ensued. I made my way home after the last few folks returned, a little hoarse from yelling, but with the happy glow of having been part of something lovely.

Almost $3.8 million dollars for 92 charities across the country was raised this year. Since 2011, the Coldest Night of the Year has raised $7.9 million dollars. The team led by Tony "the Tiger" brought in more than $19,000 for SMUN, whose overall total was just under their goal at $79,000.

March 14, 2016

#FABFEATS: NIAGARA COUNTS

As I have noted in past blogs, one of the most exciting things about my 50 Fabulous Feats is the number of interesting opportunities available to me in my own community. Having a more open and curious approach to local events means that when I come across an activity that might be a possible feat, my first reaction is "I'm in." So, when I saw a notice from the Niagara Region asking for volunteers to participate in conducting a survey called "Niagara Counts," I wanted to find out more.

Through clicking on the site link, I discovered that the survey would be a point-in-time count that would provide a snapshot of homelessness in Niagara. As part of a national strategy to help determine the extent of homelessness over 30 communities across Canada, Niagara Counts represented the first time this survey would be conducted in our community. By finding out more information about individuals who are living on the streets or in emergency shelters, it is hoped that we will learn more about people who are affected by homelessness and what their needs are in order to better serve them and, ultimately, eliminate homelessness.

Niagara's first point-in-time count was scheduled for April 5, 2016 and the Niagara Region was recruiting volunteers to assist with the process. As I read more, I learned that they were seeking volunteers to participate in the outside count; teams of 3 would be dispatched at a particular location where, between the hours of 5 – 8 in the morning, they would walk their route and survey individuals who agreed to participate, and count those who refused, or were not able to do so (for example, asleep or otherwise unable). It was noted that each team would be assigned a team lead who had experience working with people who are homeless.

Although I did not have experience working with individuals who were homeless, I felt that this survey was important for our region and decided to participate. I filled out the volunteer form and shortly received an email confirmation and notice of a training session and orientation. There were about 20 people at this session where members of the organizing group from the Niagara Region provided a very comprehensive walk through of the process and a brief safety training. The final portion of the meeting had us connecting with our other team members and role playing the survey administration in order for us to become more comfortable with the questions before the day of the count.

I made sure to reread the survey and the volunteer guide again the night before the count to make sure I was as prepared as possible. I then set my alarm for 3:30 a.m. and tried to go to sleep early. It took me some time to get to sleep, and I awoke several times during the night, each time checking the clock to make sure I hadn't slept through the alarm. I got up just ahead of the actual 3:30 alarm, and was struck by how very dark it was outside. It had turned cold over the last week, so I bundled up in extra layers knowing that we would be spending the majority of the shift outside and headed out to the check-in point for Niagara Falls. I met one of my team members in the parking lot and we entered together, signed in, picked up our survey materials, connected with our team lead, and soon we all made our way out to our various survey locations.

We were assigned to Lundy's Lane between Dorchester and Drummond. Clipboards in hand and bright orange Niagara Counts backpacks in place, we began to walk our route. In the time leading up to the count day, there had been hints of spring, but on this morning, snow covered the ground and it was cold. As a result, there were few people on the street, especially at 5 a.m. We walked the route several times, noting a few people whom we saw from a distance on our tally sheet. About half way through our shift, we entered the McDonalds to warm up with a coffee. Inside we noticed a number of people who may have been homeless. On the one hand, I was glad to know that people were not outside on such a cold morning, but, because we could not conduct the survey inside establishments, their possible information was not available to us. I was glad to know that in addition to the outside count, there was another group of individuals who were also conducting the survey in shelters.

Our time went by relatively quickly as the three of us chatted during the trek up and down the street. Our team lead told us that she and her daughter had experienced homelessness after arriving in Niagara Falls. While she was thankful for the services that found them a place to live relatively quickly, she lamented that others she had met were not as fortunate.

Around 7:30 we decided we had collected all that we could on our route and returned to the checkpoint to hand in our survey materials and sign out. While we had not had the opportunity to interview anyone, we had contributed to the information that would be used to better understand homelessness and, hopefully, be used to develop appropriate programming to support these individuals.

At home just after 8 a.m. I had a hot bath and thawed out my frozen body. I reflected on the fact that I had been outside only a short period of time, and that individuals without secure housing might spend not just hours, but days, weeks, months sleeping "rough". After a hot tea and toast, I climbed back into my warm bed where my dogs still lay sleeping soundly. I realized how privileged I was to have these luxuries, and the tenuous nature of basic human safety and security. A follow up email received the next day thanked us for our assistance and assured us that once results were summarized, we would be invited to a debriefing on the findings. While my feat may be completed, the real work is yet to be done.

April 7, 2016

PILLAR OF POSITIVITY #2:

Cultivating Optimism

If I asked people I know to describe me, I suspect many would mention my smile and a laugh that is loud, heartfelt, and contagious. In the past when I have done presentations about living with depression and anxiety, I have received comments that I don't "look like a depressed person." My response is always the same: "I'm not a depressed person, I am a happy person with a depressive disorder."

However, like everyone, I have times that are challenging, days when happiness doesn't naturally bubble to the surface. And, like many people, when I am dealing with a depressive episode, it can feel almost impossible to identify, let alone focus on, something positive. Enter the next #FabFeat "pillar of positivity" – **cultivating optimism.**

Sonja Luybormirsky describes the practice of cultivating optimism in the following way: "Finding the silver lining in a cloud. Not only celebrating the present and the past, but anticipating a bright future." I was particularly taken by this quotation as it reflects my own philosophy of life. While I cannot say that things happen for a reason given so many horrible and heartbreaking events in this world, I do believe that I can take away learning, meaning, and purpose from things that do take place; this represents the "silver lining" for me. For example, when I was downsized from my Human Resources position of 26 years, I had the opportunity to return to school, complete my Master's degree, and am now able to work in my new mental health career as a Recovery Support Worker.

The benefits of cultivating optimism are significant including increased motivation to achieve goals; more effective coping skills; positive mood; higher energy and morale.

Optimism is something that can developed and enhanced through exercises and practices. Below are few that can help you to cultivate your own silver lining:

- **The Best Possible Self:** Take about 10 minutes and write about your best possible future self: your life as you always imagined it would be, having achieved all the things you wanted to the best of your abilities. Let the writing flow. After you have finished, reflect upon how you feel. Are you inspired to make these goals and dreams come true? A variation on this practice is to write about a goal that you wish to accomplish in five years, describing it in terms of the steps you have taken to successfully get there.
- **Doors: Closed and Open:** Reflect upon a time in your life when something didn't turn

out as you had planned – a relationship, a job, a project. Now consider what happened after that particular "door" closed. What door opened to you that would not have otherwise been an option?

- **Identify Barrier Thoughts:** Increase your optimistic thinking by becoming more aware of your automatic pessimistic thoughts. For example, each time you have a negative thought, place a penny in a jar while replacing the pessimism with a more favourable thought. Since the brain cannot focus on two opposite feelings at the same time, you are training your mind toward hardwiring positivity.

Time to build our optimism muscles together.

A pessimist sees the difficulty in every opportunity; an optimist sees the opportunity in every difficulty. – Winston Churchill (who lived with bipolar disorder)

January 15, 2017

#FABFEAT: SPEAKING OUT ABOUT MENTAL HEALTH

This feat is a bit of a "cheat" since it is not a completely novel experience. I have been volunteering with the Canadian Mental Health Association – Niagara Branch Speakers' Bureau since 2008. However, for someone who lives with and speaks about mental illness, both my own and that of my older son, every talk is a feat in and of itself; two of the most difficult situations are rolled together as the inherently anxiety-producing public speaking focuses on personal stories about a very stigmatized topic.

The other novelty of this talk is its emphasis not on my experiences living with mental illness, but as the parent of a young adult son who is dealing with his diagnosis of bipolar disorder, generalized anxiety disorder, and panic disorder. It is only the second time I have spoken from this perspective; the first time was at last year's Speak OUT event that was accompanied by an article my son and I participated in for the St. Catharines Standard (http://www.stcatharinesstandard.ca/2014/10/22/mom-students-to-talk-about-mental-illness). In the year since that article was published, we have continued our journey together, punctuated by ups and downs along the way.

The other part of the feat was that I was given the privilege to present as part of a panel of courageous, amazing students who told their own stories of challenges with mental illness including depression, anxiety, bipolar disorder, and obsessive-compulsive disorder. In advance of the evening event, the four of us met and shared a little about our experiences and I felt an immediate kinship with them. Brett and Steph are undergraduate students who, despite significant challenges, convey a message of positivity, hope, and resilience. Lauren, a fellow graduate student at Brock, was someone I knew from participating in her Master's research about individuals living well with mental illness. She is currently working on her PhD in the area, further exploring the model she developed in her Master's thesis in partnership with the mental health unit at the Niagara Health System. She is also a participant in her own research, living with her own mental illness.

The event included a short presentation from each of us about our experiences, a panel discussion answering some common questions about stigma and stress as well as ideas regarding how to support family, friends, or colleagues who may be dealing with mental health challenges and, how to maintain self-care in these supportive roles. Questions from the audience and the online viewers rounded out the night.

Reading this blog, you might wonder why anyone would choose to expose their personal struggles to 100 strangers (not to mention the faceless audience who joined us through online live stream). My fellow presenters expressed reasons that mirror my own: if one person can be reassured, supported, encouraged to seek help, or just feel less alone as a result of hearing our stories, we are more than compensated for any discomfort we may feel. I was especially impressed by the maturity displayed by these students in their 20's and early 30's who were, as I told them, decades ahead of me in their ability to embrace their mental health challenges and work to help others.

The end of the night was punctuated by individuals who approached us to thank us for speaking out; they shared their own stories – some tears were shed, and many hugs given and received.

As I walked to my car, I called Christian to tell him about the experience. I told him that I had updated my speech just before the presentation to include the most recent update to our journey which had occurred the very morning of the event when Christian decided he was ready to access supports through the Canadian Mental Health Association – Niagara Branch. The smile on his face when he emerged from his intake meeting was the only confirmation I needed to reaffirm that the timing of events is often not coincidental. As I told the audience, it was a new ray of hope in a world where we must never give up hope.

I am dedicating this feat to Brett, Steph, and Lauren who reminded me that the courage of good people is all we need to change the world. For those who may not have had the opportunity to attend or watch Speak OUT online, the recorded event is available at: http://brockvideocentre.brocku.ca/videos/video/189/

November 6, 2016

#FABFEAT: JUST A PAUSE; NOT THE END

For or those who have read my previous posts, you will know that, in addition to my own challenges, my older son lives with mental illness. While we have both been stretched at different times in our ability to cope with these circumstances, I truly believe that we are also more closely connected because of our shared struggles.

I recognize that Christian's illness likely results, in part, because of a genetic predisposition, and have experienced my fair share of "Mom guilt" because of this fact. Yet, I know that our closeness has also been cemented by the various mental health trials and tribulations that we have journeyed through together. And, while CJ has accompanied me on a few of my fabulous feats so far, this week's adventure holds a special significance for me because it is something that acknowledges and celebrates our connection through mental illness.

This feat is inspired by The Semicolon Project. In 2013, Amy Bleuel wanted to pay tribute to her father, whom she had lost to suicide. Amy adopted the semicolon as a symbol to promote discussion around mental illness. The tattoo of a semicolon represents a sentence the author could have ended, but chose not to. Amy's message is that that we are all authors, and the sentence we choose to continue, after taking a pause, is our lives. Since its beginnings, the

Semicolon Project has become a global movement (www.projectsemicolon.org) that represents hope and love for those who struggle with mental illness, suicide, addiction, and self-injury.

When I first heard about the semicolon symbol, I loved the idea. For both Christian and me, there have been pauses in life, times when the sentence might well have ended, but, thankfully, did not. Appreciating and celebrating this victory, especially together, seemed to me like a feat well worth pursuing. So, when I had my nose pierced, we decided to inquire about the semicolon tattoo and within a few weeks had booked our appointments at Artistic Impressions.

I already had a tattoo, having foreseen my 50 fabulous feats a few years earlier with the occasional mid-life adventure. On my 46th birthday, I got a frog tattoo on my ankle. As my spirit animal, the frog represented transition and it is very special to me. It also allowed me to dictate to my boys that I supported their own decisions around getting tattoos, and they could do so, like me, as soon as they turned 46.

However, I broke my own rule by taking my 23-year-old son to get his first tattoo. We both filled out our paperwork and then CJ sat down to begin the process for getting a one-inch semicolon on his inner right wrist. The tattoo looked great on his wrist, but when it came to be my turn, I wondered if it was too big for my arm, which is much smaller than his. When I asked our tattooist if I could get mine a size smaller, he smiled and said, "you can, but if you're getting a tattoo, get a tattoo." I realized it was time to put my money where my mouth was, as my Mom would have said. If stigma and discrimination elimination was important to me, then I had to be willing to step up and play my part. And so, the choice was "go big or go home." I sat in the chair and received my own semicolon, bold, black, and beautiful, on my forearm.

Christian and I topped off the afternoon with lunch and occasional comparisons of our matching tattoos: a concrete illustration of the connections in our chemical brains as well as our emotional hearts. While CJ is talking about what his next "tat" will be, I think I'm done for now. But, I'm happy to have a feat that will be with me for a lifetime, that visibly celebrates my ability to live well with mental illness, and connects me to my beautiful boy in a way that is so much more than skin-deep.

March 18, 2016

#FABFEATS: MEETING BARBARA

Sometimes I think the Universe is lending me a helping hand in pursuing my Fabulous Feats. This was the case when I ran across a post on Facebook for The Canadian Positive Psychology Association and discovered that their conference was taking place in June at White Oaks, Niagara-on-the-Lake. At that time, I was still in search of work and so inquired about volunteering to reduce the cost of my registration. The result was becoming an Ambassador for the three-day event that included some of the biggest names in positive psychology research: Caroline Miller, David Cooperrider, and, I could hardly believe my luck, Barbara Fredrickson.

Of course, life also has a way of making things just a bit more complicated than we anticipate and between my registration and the conference, I was privileged enough to be hired to work for Niagara Region Mental Health. I had several commitments I had made prior to beginning work and had already taken time off for my convocation, and needed three days for a trip to Ottawa (stay tuned for my SPARKie adventures in future blogs) the week after the conference so taking a full three days off for the conference was a bit challenging (thank you for hiring me, do you mind if I take half the month of June off?). My Manager and team were stars, though, allowing me to pick up an extra weekend of work so I could use my days off to attend.

I had been assigned to the registration desk which meant I needed to be at White Oaks Resort by 6:45 on the first two days. I was excited to be able to attend sessions after morning registration and before the pre-conference check-ins on the first evening. I enjoyed meeting the participants and was giddy after attending sessions on such topics as appreciative inquiry, mindfulness, and grit. At the end of one workshop, when each participant was sharing what we would take away with us, I ridiculously blurted out "I found my tribe!" which was met with laughter and delighted affirmations from others in the room.

On the second day, I looked forward to being able to slip away from the registration desk in time to hear one of my rock star researchers, Barbara Fredrickson, deliver the keynote. I felt especially excited because Dr. Fredrickson's Broaden and Build Theory is foundational to my own growth over the last couple of years. She posits that positive emotions like joy, contentment, and love, help people to be open to new ideas (broaden) that, in turn, allows individuals to grow their physical, intellectual, and social resources (build). Her research has provided strong support that positive emotions broaden one's awareness and encourage novel, varied, and exploratory thoughts and actions that build skills and resources which can be drawn on later for coping and resilience. I feel that my own positive focus has been the driving force for my own psychological growth and my ability to bounce back in the face of challenges. Further, in my new position working with individuals living with severe mental illness, I feel that broaden and build can provide a means by which narrow and limiting focuses on negative emotions can be improved through opening to the power of building wellbeing through small positive thoughts and actions.

It is at this point that the Universe interceded again: one of the room monitors was absent and I was asked to take over the duties. This meant I was relieved of registration duties and found myself able to arrive early for Dr. Fredrickson's keynote. I picked a seat right in front of the podium and was so excited. I would see my research hero up close. As I scanned the room, I noticed a woman sitting alone at the table next to me. I quickly realized it was HER! Drawing on my broaden and build resources, I surprised myself by walking right over to her and introducing myself. I told her of how much her research has meant to me personally and how I felt I could bring it to the clients with whom I was now working. She was gracious and humble; she thanked me for sharing my experiences and told me that because she did not work with clinical populations, she was grateful when others shared their stories and especially related to taking the research to those whom it could help the most. She shook my hand and I returned to my seat.

Barbara's keynote was amazing: she talked about prioritizing positivity and the importance of interpersonal micro-moments of positivity that open everything from our physical posture to our ability to consider different possibilities, ideas, and relationships. I left her talk buoyed by both the message and the messenger.

I completed my duties as Ambassador introducing speakers in several sessions and thanking them for their contributions. At the final keynote, the volunteers were brought on stage and, in turn, thanked for our efforts. I felt incredibly grateful for the opportunity to play even a small role in this tremendous event. Thanks to all who brought the CPPA into my world (Universe included).

July 3, 2016

#FABFEATS: IT'S ALL ABOUT THE STORY

The Niagara Falls History Museum was the site of my latest feat. Located in the old Stamford Town Hall on Ferry Street, it received a 12-million-dollar renovation in 2012 in order to properly preserve and house its more than 26,000 artifacts. I am embarrassed to say that in all the years I have lived in Niagara Falls, I have never visited the museum. When Culture Days advertised a behind the scenes tour, I decided it was time to check it out.

Since my older son, Christian, had been having some challenges with his mood as is not uncommon as Fall sets in, I gently cajoled him into accompanying me to change up his day by being around, but not overwhelmed by, a few other folks. When we arrived, we met a lovely woman who was at the welcome desk. As Maja had us sign us up for the tour, I told her about my positive psychology experiment. She asked if I did mental health-related training and shared that it would be especially helpful for museum front-line staff who regularly encounter individuals presenting with unusual behaviours and other challenges, possibly related to ongoing mental illness. I talked about a presentation for the Welland Public Library staff that I had participated in with Canadian Mental Health Association workers and suggested something similar could be arranged. We exchanged information, and Maja said that she would talk to her Manager and get back to me. It was only when I began to write this blog that I realized the Culture and Museum Manager is someone I know through his wife and mother, both of whom I worked with at Brock University. Once again, it seems to me that the Universe has chosen to send its intentions my way.

While we waited for the tour, Christian and I browsed the War of 1812 gallery. Given the opportunity to don a coatee and hat, and brandish a musket, I dutifully hammed it up for the camera. It made my kid laugh too, which was a good thing. Returning to the reception area, about 8 other people were waiting as Christine, our guide, joined us to begin the tour. We were quite a heterogeneous group: Christian and me, several middle-aged women, an elderly couple, a Dad and his young daughter. Christine took us to the elevator and we descended to the basement storage area. She explained to us that their recent renovations had allowed the museum to properly store the variety of pieces – from ploughs to chairs to pictures to taxidermized animals and birds. My favourite was Skipper, a dog born without front legs whose owner had fashioned a wheeled apparatus, so he could get around on his own. After his death (from natural causes we were assured), the owner, who was a taxidermist, mounted both Skipper and his skeleton, which were preserved for future generations like us to see.

Christine explained that for years the museum had collected items with an emphasis on breadth rather than depth. As a result, many of the artifacts have little history attached to them. The mandate now is all about "telling the story and preserving the ongoing culture and history of Niagara Falls." Later, in the War of 1812 exhibit, she illustrated this concept using as an example a small scrap of material that became part of the collection. Through research and enhanced preservation techniques, this piece of crumpled uniform was restored and identified by the type of wool and buttons used to be that of an officer; a further investigation found two officers who had died in this battle. This item now tells its important and personal story to the visitors of the museum about the War of 1812 through a real soldier's experience.

When Christian asked Christine about her favourite artifact, she shared another significant element to the museum's content: it's not just about old items; the culture and community of Niagara Falls encompasses both old and new and is meant to tell the story for generations to come. Christine enjoyed the materials associated with the daredevils, including Nick Wallenda's 2012 walk "over the mighty Niagara Falls" as is captioned in the signed poster displayed upstairs. I gravitated to an interactive exhibit that allowed visitors to try their own hand (or more appropriately, feet) at traversing the Falls on a tightrope. My silly antics again received laughs from the boy, who was easily coaxed into taking my picture.

As we arrived back in the lobby area, we again saw Maja who reconfirmed her interest in connecting about mental health training in the future. We also picked up brochures advertising upcoming activities at the museums including a community yoga series and a Fall film series (programmed by another former Brock colleague, the amazing Joan Nicks). As we left, Christian commented that he was surprised how much he had enjoyed the afternoon and expressed interest in checking out the yoga program as well. For my part, I happily noted how anecdotally we had demonstrated the idea that novel, intentional activities, laughter, and social connections can have a positive impact on one's mood. Another Fabulous Feat successfully completed, with a dash of mental health education sprinkled in for good measure.

October 3, 2016

PILLAR OF WELLNESS #3:
Practicing Acts Of Kindness

Having just come through the long, grey days of January, I think it is forgivable for us to be more focused on self-preservation than engaging in acts of kindness. I have witnessed more short tempers than I have selfless acts in support of others and confess that I may have contributed less than positive vibes sometimes too. Maybe that's just the reason we all need this month's #FabFeat "pillar of positivity" – **practicing acts of kindness.**

The wonderful part about practicing acts of kindness is that not only does it improve the lives of those you help, it has also been found to benefit you as the giver of kindness. This isn't surprising - everyone can think of a time when they experienced that warm glow after assisting another, be they friend or stranger. Recently, research into acts of kindness have provided more information about how best to maximize the positive outcomes. For instance, when the acts are performed together, they provide the giver with greater joy. When the kinds of activities are varied, the benefits are again multiplied as we become less acclimated to doing the same thing all the time.

Performing acts of kindness also has a positive impact on our perception of ourselves as compassionate people resulting in feeling more useful, confident, and optimistic. In turn, others are inspired by our example making practicing acts of kindness a contagious activity; you can help others reap the benefits of kindness in a "pay it forward" kind of upward spiral.

I have always been the kind of person who wants to support others. I am an avid volunteer and intuitively know when someone needs a little TLC. My 50 Feats adventures allowed me to find new ways to practice this pillar, from building a playground to planting trees to working with kindergarten kids learning about science.

Each activity provided me with yet another benefit of practicing acts of kindness: social connection. I fondly remember the conversation I had with the Motts employee from Georgia who had immigrated to the States and was thrilled to be able to give back by building the playground as part of their corporate initiative. I smile as I think about the expressions of awe on the faces of those little scientists as I played marine biologist Sue holding up the octopus and learning as much from them as they did from me. Interestingly, these acts cost me exactly zero dollars; my time and interest were the only assets I needed to bring to the table.

Practicing acts of kindness can be easily included in your daily activities. Below are few ideas that might "jump start" your practice:

Random Acts of Kindness: Think about how you might engage in a few small (or large) acts every week. Track them in a journal to remind yourself of these activities and reflect on how it felt to help someone else.

Spending Money on Others: This activity doesn't involve a lot of money. Research has found that spending as little as five dollars on others can increase your (and their) happiness levels. Buy coffee for the person behind you in the drive through, leave a five-dollar bill in your favourite book at the bookstore for the person who buys it, smile and say hello to a stranger. It's just that simple.

Random Acts of Kindness week runs from February 12 – 17, 2017. Visit https://randomactsof.us/ for more information and join me in sharing your own ACTS OF KINDNESS.

"Too often we underestimate the power of a touch, a smile, a kind word, a listening ear, an honest compliment, or the smallest act of caring, all of which have the potential to turn a life around."
– Leo Buscaglia

February 13, 2017

#FABFEAT: IT'S IN YOU TO GIVE

I am a little embarrassed to say that I have never donated blood. As a young adult, I was diagnosed with ulcerative colitis and, as a result of frequent flare-ups, was very thin. When I considered giving blood at that time, I was under the weight requirement. I didn't think much about it again until I began to create my 50 feats list and wanted to have some that involved giving back to my community.

According to Canadian Blood Services (blood.ca), 50% of Canadians will need blood, or know someone else who does, at some point in their lives. Yet, only 4% of Canadians actually donate. Given that my blood type, A negative, is shared by only 4% of the population, I was even more excited about being able to help someone in need through my blood donation.

I signed up for a clinic that was at a local church. When I arrived, I was surprised by the number of cars in the parking lot and even more so when I entered – the church hall was alive with people. A friendly volunteer named Janet gave me a number and, while I waited, I chatted with her about this being my first time giving blood. She enthusiastically thanked me for choosing to donate.

My first stop was to have a small blood sample taken from my finger to check my iron level. A lovely, young woman explained the process to me as she worked, all the while smiling despite the numerous hours she had already laboured. A quick check showed that my iron level was within the normal range.

Having passed the first test (since achieving the weight minimum was clearly not a stumbling block for me anymore), up next was a questionnaire regarding my health. While I waited for my number to be called this time, I was entertained by a little, blonde girl who had accompanied her parents to the clinic. She danced, and skipped about under the watchful eyes of her Mom and Dad, and for those of us awaiting our turn, she brought smiles to our faces and made the time fly.

It was quickly my turn; a lovely nurse ushered me into a cubical and took my blood pressure and pulse before reviewing my questionnaire with me. I chatted with the nurse as she performed the tests, explaining my 50 Feats at 50 adventures and why I had chosen donating blood as one of my "firsts". She said she was inspired by the idea, that perhaps she would put together her own list.

When we got to the question regarding Crohn's disease, I explained that I had ulcerative colitis, but that it was well controlled with maintenance drugs. She consulted her manual and showed me the section on ulcerative colitis that excluded donations from those using medication. While the reason I take medication is to reduce the potential of flare-ups, it meant that I was ineligible to donate. The nurse explained that the standard was in place protect my health. Every person has approximately 5 litres of blood and 450 ml is collected in one donation; the loss of nearly $1/10^{th}$ of a person's blood volume can cause a strain on the body which is not a problem for most healthy people, but could negatively impact my disease.

The nurse was incredibly supportive and took time to fully explain my situation. The standards do sometimes change over time, so she suggested there was a chance I could give in the future. She proposed another way of fulfilling my feat: by encouraging friends and family to donate.

As I left the building, I reflected on my situation. I was disappointed to not be able to donate. But, I recognize that not everything works out in life the way we plan. I am the poster child for events taking a different kind of a turn; yet, I am also the greatest proponent of boldly taking that left turn and seeing where it leads -it's part of the adventure.

While my feat did not end with my blood donation, it did give me insight into the many people in my community who do choose to give back through their regular donations, by volunteering their time to make the whole experience possible, and educating people like me about the process. Everyone I met was encouraging, warm, and sincerely thankful for the opportunity to give and receive.

My feat began with an intention to give blood, but perhaps the feat that I was meant to perform was to illustrate for others how beautiful giving the gift of life can be. There was a glow in that clinic hall from all the smiling faces and I could feel the warmth of every open heart (okay, there was a heat wave, but I believe it was the good karma).

I hope that, like the kind nurse suggested, by sharing my experience, I might inspire someone else – or maybe a few others – to donate. If you do, I send you my heartfelt thanks in the knowledge that my 3rd feat has been completed vicariously through my community of connections.

August 3, 2016

#FABFEAT: KABOOM! IT'S A PLAYGROUND

When I began to identify my 50 feats, I purposefully wanted to include some volunteer activities that allow me to give back to my wonderful community. So, when I received a notice that the Heritage Park Playground Build Committee was seeking volunteers for their community build day, I was eager to sign up. I didn't know much more about it other than there was a need for a large number of volunteers and that I was to wear comfortable clothes and closed-toed shoes. Since there was no call for work boots I thought it was likely safe to assume they weren't seeking skilled labour and, as my son (who knows my construction skill level) suggested, probably needed someone to hand out water to the real workers.

I arrived at 8:00 a.m. to find numerous volunteers already registered and the playing field separated into work stations – mulch pile towering at the edge, equipment pieces ready for assembly, skids of sod ready to roll (out). We all enjoyed a coffee, then, donning our "Let's PLAY" volunteer shirts, were assigned to our project group based on the sticker on our name tags. I was an apple and joined a group of high school seniors from Grimsby and their teacher.

At the work station we were met by some City of Niagara Falls maintenance workers also assigned to our group. Our task was to assemble two benches and a table, which sounds easy until they showed us the boards that needed to be measured, drilled with precision holes that fit the steel frames, and bolted together. They brought out the power drills, T-squares and levels; it was at this point that it became clear to me that my group assignment had been a random act in no way based upon my skill sets.

The City employees, Dan and John, seeing my obvious discomfort, and wishing to avoid all the accident forms that would surely result from placing a power tool in my hands, suggested I could paint the railings where the new Heritage Park sign would be hung, and ensured further avoidance of potential liability by sending their colleague Corey along with me. While we painted (I did the bottom half where mistakes were less likely to be noticed), the other groups worked their magic and, little by little, the playground equipment was assembled, placed into each designated area, and skillfully cemented into place. By 10:00 a.m. I could hardly believe the progress; It seems that 400 hands make light work.

As I talked to other volunteers throughout the day I learned more about the project. The community build was a joint venture made possible by a Build it with KaBOOM Playground Grant that the City of Niagara Falls had received. KaBOOM is a non-profit organization that believes the well-being of society depends upon the well-being of its children, and that all kids deserve an opportunity for active play; quite simply, Play Matters (https://kaboom.org/play_matters). The successful grant allowed the City to be partnered with Canada Dry Mott's (and its parent company Dr. Pepper Snapple Group) who paid for the $140,000 project. In addition, over 100 employees of Canada Dry Mott's, who were attending a conference in Niagara Falls, came out to participate in the build along with City and community volunteers. The project would honestly have not been accomplished without these amazing partnerships.

In addition to painting, I took my turn at shoveling mulch into tarps that were dragged onto the playground. It was hard work and I was so impressed with the array of dedicated men and women who spent hours under the hot sun moving the mountain of mulch onto the equipment area.

At the entrance, another group of volunteers displayed their creative flair, painting the walkway with colourful flowers and rainbows, Canadian flags, four squares, hop scotch and snakes and ladders games. The children from the adjacent school, Victoria Park, took turns having their hands painted and pressed onto the path, leaving their own special legacies. One beaming volunteer named Mohammed from Mott's in Mississauga told me his day was made by a little girl who told him that she liked the fish he was painting. "That's what this is all about and I'm so happy to be able to help" he smiled.

Looking around, it was clear that everyone shared that feeling.

With more than 200 volunteers, we finished early – the whole 1,500-square-foot playground was completed in 6 hours! We were joined again by the Victoria Park children, who sang us a song, participated in the ribbon cutting, and gave each volunteer a handwritten thank you card as we departed. Mine reads "Dear volunteer, I am SO glad that you are bilding the park. I am going to have so much fun on it when its bild. From Trayton." There could be no better payment for the day's work than these postcards. I know that Trayton, and all his friends, will have many hours of enjoyment and, whenever I drive by, I will feel just a little bit of pride at having been a small part of creating such a wonderful playground in our community.

September 25, 2016

#FABFEAT: SCIENTIST SUE

My boys are now 23 and almost 20, so I am at that point in my life where I have limited opportunities to be around little children. While I admit I enjoy the freedom that comes with having young adult sons, I sometimes miss the wonder of their imaginations when they were small. So, when my friend Karen invited me to attend one of her Scientist in School workshops with a local junior/senior kindergarten class, I jumped at the chance.

Walking into the classroom, I was struck by how small everything was – the chairs, the tables, the kids! As part of the program, there were several areas that the children would travel around to over the hour including a chemistry, astronomy, paleontology, and weather centre. There were two parents who were volunteering for the morning. The young woman sitting closest to me tentatively asked if I had a child in the class; with a chuckle, I explained to her that my kids were grown, that I was a friend of Karen's.

My wonderful friend, Scientist Karen, gave me the best centre to oversee: the marine biologist station. I quickly read my instructions for my role as Scientist Sue. There was a table covered with shells and what I came to know were sea stars (not star fish as I would have called them since they don't have bones like fish – my learning continues) as well as magnifying glasses. Another station had rubber fish that the children would roll paint onto and then cover with paper to form a fish fossil. Finally, the pièce de résistance, three real (dead) octopi that could be touched, held, and explored.

Karen is a retired elementary school teacher and as she sat with the class at the beginning of the workshop explaining the morning ahead, I understood why she is so warmly greeted by former students every time we are out together. She is an exceptional teacher! Karen managed to connect with the kids immediately. She asked questions of the tiny soon-to-be scientists, ensured that both the eager sharers and the more reticent children all had opportunities to contribute, and genuinely praised their ideas and suggestions.

Each student was then assigned to groups of 3 or 4 and directed to their first station. Four little people (two boys and two girls) joined me at the observation table and sat with me on the ridiculously small chairs (to be fair, the chairs were perfectly sized for everyone but me). While two students inspected the shells and plastic marine animals with magnifying glasses, the other two moved to the painting table where they made their fish fossils. They then switched places, so everyone had a turn at both centres.

In the last few minutes, the four excitedly stood close to me as I opened the container holding the octopi and held one in my hand. There were gasps and giggles as they tentatively touched the octopus (in truth, many of the giggles were mine); a few even held it in outstretched hands. They looked at the tentacles, commented on how it felt (slimy, cold, bumpy), and smelled (yucky).

When we heard the gong that signaled the end of their time in the first area, the kids followed instructions to push in their chairs, and repeated with Scientist Karen: "stand up and breath, it's time to leave." They took two deep breaths (as modeled by Karen, in through the nose, out through the mouth) to prepare their "scientist brains", then, after pointing in the direction they would be going, walked quietly to the next station. I was impressed by how effortlessly Karen incorporated mindful breathing into the activity, and how quickly the kids adopted the techniques.

I had five sets of kids over the course of the morning. Even though it had been a while since I had spent the morning with 4 and 5-year old's, after I had finished one round, I got into the groove and was able to simply enjoy the moments. I laughed at the different reactions each child had to the octopus, marveled at the little blonde girl who complimented her classmate on his "really good fish picture," and enjoyed engaging with both the outgoing and more reserved children.

The end of the workshop saw the little scientists sitting on the carpet with Karen leading them through questions about what they had learned.

Just as she had incorporated breathing techniques into the station transitions, Karen used the science to introduce a bit of yoga, having the children stretch out their arms like sea stars. While I realize that these kids were particularly well behaved, I also know that Karen's calm approach and mindful tools supported their self-regulation during the morning's activities.

Later that day I showed my younger son the picture of me holding the octopus for the children to see. He said I looked like the most excited kid there; he wasn't wrong. However, even though I had an enormous amount of fun, being with small children took significant energy and I confess to being pretty exhausted for the rest of the day. I gained a newfound respect for teachers who do this job all day, every day and a great appreciation for teachers like Scientist Karen who support and encourage every child's growth and development.

January 25, 2016

#FABFEAT: REDUCING MY CARBON FOOTPRINT

You can't turn on the news these days without hearing about the dire state of our environment, especially related to climate change. It is hard to believe it is still a topic being debated when all the science points to the almost irretrievable world situation.

While there are lots of people who spend their time talking and lamenting, there are also those that dig in (pun intended) and do something about it. My latest feat allowed me to spend a morning with a group of local eco-heroes making their positive difference in the world: Greening Niagara (greeningniagara.ca).

Greening Niagara (GN) began in 2006 as Climate Action Niagara and currently provides eco-education in action to foster lifestyle changes that support heathier, resilient communities and reduced carbon footprints. As a volunteer-driven, non-profit organization, Greening Niagara collaborates with community stakeholders (municipalities, businesses, school boards, faith-based organizations, and other non-profits and charities) in community initiatives that positively impact our environment. These programs include community gardens, gardening and canning workshops, eco-speakers and film series, and an annual one-day event called Eco-Fest Niagara.

I had the privilege of joining the GN volunteers for their autumn planning day. This was my first experience with tree planting other than for my own landscaping at home. I was aware that trees reduce our carbon footprint by absorbing carbon dioxide to produce oxygen, but I also learned that planting trees that are native to an area support and preserve the environment and its biodiversity.

Our planting area was along Merritt Trail in St. Catharines. Despite living in Niagara for almost 30 years, I wasn't familiar with the pathway. The Welland Canal Society built the trail, which was completed in 1986. It begins in south St. Catharines at Bradley Street and stretches through to Martindale Road in the west. The trail is bicycle, dog-walking, and pedestrian-friendly, although, the 11 kilometres are not continuous so it is recommended that walkers download a map before starting out (http://www. stcatharines.ca/en/playin/MerrittTrail.asp).

I wasn't sure what to expect when I arrived, but it was a crisp, sunny day and I knew that, if nothing else, I would enjoy being outside on a beautiful Fall morning. I met the tireless Executive Director, Jane Hanlon, as she headed out to place signs directing the volunteers to the site. My first task was to watch for the trees that Land Care Niagara Stewardship Coordinator, Olivia, was delivering for planting.

I spent the next two hours along with about a dozen other volunteers getting the maple and tulip trees introduced to their new homes. I worked with Olivia untangling two beautiful, root-bound tulip trees from their plastic pots. During this time, I also watched and listened to the others as the worked. From one volunteer, I learned about the problems with the clay soil that we were planting in that necessitated an infusion of richer soil in order for the trees to prosper. Jane showed us how to make vertical cuts around the root mass in order to disrupt the roots that were spiraled and compacted by the pot before placing them in the freshly dug holes.

I learned that several of the volunteers were Brock University students who were in various programs – Recreation and Leisure Studies, Concurrent Education, Applied Disabilities Studies (accompanied by a young woman with whom she was working) and Public Health (completing an internship with GN). In addition, there were community members interested in giving back and improving their region- some were long-term volunteers with GN; others, like me, were brand new to the group. The energy from the group was contagious, with lots of laughing and talking amid the digging and planting.

All the trees were planted by noon and we returned to our homes and to our own various Saturday afternoon activities. I drove home with the smell of Fall in my hair and rich black soil under my nails. Another fantastic feat accomplished with multiple positive results: a couple of hours of sunshine, exercise, and good company; the opportunity to make my community a little eco-friendlier; and the discovery of a brand-new place to go with my buddies, Murphy (my Golden-Doodle), his friend Ted (my Shih-Tzu), and their frequent companion Keane (The Navigator's Jack Russell Terrier mix) – winners all around!

October 22, 2015

PILLAR OF POSITIVITY #4:
Nurturing Social Relationships

I am an introvert by nature, though some might puzzle about how an introvert can be so darn loud! I definitely need my alone time to recharge my batteries, but I also know that I am at my best when surrounded by people I love. That's not surprising; humans are wired for connection. However, when my anxiety and depression sneak in, I can find myself turning down invitations, making excuses, ensuring that my world becomes smaller and smaller. I know from my work with individuals living with mental illness, conversations with others who also have challenges with their mental health, and my own personal experience that one of the common threads we share is the tendency to socially isolate when we are unwell. It is for this reason that this wellness pillar is so important to me: **nurturing social relationships.**

There is significant research into the benefits of social connections. Growing our relationships with others can strengthen the immune system; provide for a longer life; lower levels of anxiety and depression; increase empathy and self-esteem. Additionally, it has been found that social connection is bi-directional: people with strong social relationships are happy and happy people are more likely to acquire friends.

I am truly blessed in my life to have incredible family and friends. During my initial 50 Feats experiment, I purposefully reached out to those around me to join me in some of my adventure; I called these outings "feats with friends" and the value came as much, if not more, from the people as from the activity. From horseback riding with one of my dearest friends to meeting kindred spirits at the Writer's Circle to simply enjoying a movie with my son, the experience – and my outlook – were enhanced by the presence of others. For those adventures that I embarked on independently, I was thrilled to meet and learn about other participants. While we began the walk downtown, night of music, or cooking class as strangers, we parted ways having shared a laugh, a story or two, and a connection.

As the warmer weather comes teasingly closer each day, why not make a "spring year's resolution" to reach out and purposely nurture your own social connections, be they old friends or potential pals-to-be.

> *"We are biologically, cognitively, physically,*
> *and spiritually wired to love, to be loved,*
> *and to belong." – Brene Brown*

March 12, 2017

#FABFEAT: AT A SNAIL'S PACE

After the physicality of my last adventure walking around the Isle of Wight, I decided that this feat needed to be just a little slower – in fact, you might say, at a snail's pace. Growing up in a home where exotic cuisine meant adding paprika to the top of the deviled eggs, my hesitation to try "different" foods was ingrained in me early. So, when I was developing my list of novel experiences, I decided there had to be at least one eating-related adventure.

Thanks to my good friend Liz, I discovered the location for my feat once again in my own backyard: Paris Crepes Café (http://www.pariscrepescafe.com/) on Queen Street in Niagara Falls. I was also excited to extend my alliteration this time to include Feats with Friends and Family as my older son joined in the fun along with Liz, Les, and Lee-Anne (you can see how this group was meant to be, can't you?).

While the feat involved my first taste of escargot, the experience was so much more. The bistro was amazing – the décor was charming, and we were greeted by the lovely Manager Starr who was also our server for our lunchtime adventure. She was a complete delight, immediately catching on to the silliness of our group experience and easily joining us on the journey.

There was much laughter and fun (apologies to the other diners there for a quiet lunch) and, yes, I ordered their Escargot Bouguignons En Croute (puff pastry crusted snails in garlic butter). They were almost too beautiful to eat, but we shared the snails among us. Even my son, whose culinary upbringing was not dissimilar to my own with regard to exotic choices, joined in.

My verdict: the snail itself wasn't what dazzled my taste buds – I suspect that is the point of all the garlic butter and pastry. We enjoyed the rest of our meal (French onion soup, delicious crepes), watched Les mourn the disappearance of his much-too-small Crème Brule and I enjoyed French press coffee, all the while chatting, laughing, and simply having the best time together.

As the only patrons left as the mid-day closing time approached, we had the opportunity to chat more with Starr, learning about her return to school for veterinary training, her love of cats, and current foster kittens; photos and stories were exchanged and enjoyed (even my dog-lover heart melted at the pictures of her tiny feline treasures).

I definitely declare this feat a rousing success. Akin to the snails, made extra special by the accompanying ingredients in their dish, this feat was fabulous because of my surroundings: a beautiful sunny afternoon in a lovely café with good friends and family sharing laughter and a meal. Honestly, who could ask for more?

September 2, 2015

#FABFEAT: JUST HORSIN' AROUND

Last week I wasn't sure what my next feat would be. Part of the fun of this adventure is that some activities are planned well in advance, while others can just happen in the moment. This week's feat fell somewhere in the middle.

My friend Annamarie and I turned 50 within a month of each other (I am younger by 21 days). At an age when having more 'stuff' isn't as appealing as accumulating experiences, we both decided that part of our celebration of the half century mark would be enjoying a variety of activities, some of which we had in common. I have never been horseback riding, so that was one for me; Annamarie wanted to take a ride from Queenston Heights to Niagara-On-The-Lake. While we couldn't quite score the location, she did find a lovely place in Port Colborne called HorsePlay Niagara that offered trail riding through the woods and along the Fort Erie beach, and invited me to join her as a birthday present.

Half the adventure was getting there; the only thing potentially worse than having me as the driver is assigning me with the role of navigator. Thankfully, my friend is both patient and has a great sense of humour, and so we arrived at our destination still smiling, *despite* my helpful directions ("I think that *was* where we were supposed to turn").

We signed our waivers, reviewed the "do not's" (which included not putting on makeup while riding – apparently a real-life example from a previous ride) and picked out our riding helmets.

I love animals, but I have never ridden a horse before, so I was equally nervous and excited about how I would find the experience. There were five others in the group and we were all lined up and assigned our animal partners based on our "horse sense". My friend and one of the men had some riding experience, but the rest of us were newbies. Lucky for me the guide knew just the horse for me and I was led to a lovely chestnut coloured beauty named Pal. He let me climb the step stool and onto his back, standing quietly in place, moving only to swipe at the flies buzzing around him. I introduced myself and rubbed Pal's neck. When we were lined up to go out on the trail, Pal fell into step behind Annamarie's horse, Mike.

We followed the trail guide, Ashley, over fields, through woods, around stiles, and across streets. While my friend's mount made numerous attempts to stop and graze along the way, my Pal was to horseback riding what Google is to cars: he knew every turn, each stop, and every trot, without need of even a twitch of the rein by me.

I was so appreciative of his skill that I kept patting his neck and telling him what a good horse he was, especially when I surprisingly remained on his back at the end of each attempt at trotting. Anyone who thinks that horseback riding is not a physical activity is wrong, and probably knows how to ride decidedly better than I do. Our guide told us it was best to stand in the stirrups and move with the horse, but I didn't manage this very well. Each time Pal sped up, I turned into some kind of cartoon character bobbing up and down wildly, holding on for dear life. My Pal didn't let me down, though, and I was grateful for his skill and my luck at having him.

The highlight for me was riding along the beach, and taking the horses out into the lake. It was a hot, sunny day and there is something about the view from high up on my gentle giant that made the adventure just a little surreal. Returning to the stable area, I gave Pal a pat on the neck and a heartfelt thank you before de-horsing. I was a little wobbly getting my land legs back, but beaming from the incredible adventure.

I'm still enjoying the memories (and some aches and pains) as I write about my latest feat, made better by having my friend Annamarie and my Pal along for the ride. And, now I totally understand why John Wayne walked that way.

September 20, 2015

#FABFEAT: THE FORCE WAS WITH ME!

I have to admit right off the bat that I never was a super Star Wars fan. Yes, I saw the originals when they came out in the late '70's and early '80's, and I did like them, but I didn't return to the theatre again and again like some folks I knew.

When the new trilogy came out more than two decades later, it was my children who drew me back and I enjoyed both the old and the new movies through little boys' eyes. On top of watching the movies (over and over), thanks again to my sons, I got to play with all the Star Wars toys: every movie character (Jabba the Hut was my favourite), and a few incredible models – the Millennium Falcon and a giant Walker were especially great – that we used to relive movie scenes as well as create our own adventures.

It is amazing how fun and freeing it was to set aside the real world for a short time and live in my sons' Star Wars universe where we could do anything, be anyone, suspend logic and even defy the laws of gravity if we so chose. I remember the conversations that took place between characters, and the sparkle in my older son's eyes when he escaped in the Falcon; I can hear the giggle of his younger brother who, though invariably relegated to play supporting characters, was beyond excited to be part of his brother's world.

For Halloween one year, both boys dressed up as Jedi Knights, complete with light sabers and "rat-tails' braids like Anakin Skywalker. I think I had as much, if not more, fun than they did watching their antics throughout the day. Alas, I don't believe I dressed up that year, a Jabba outfit being a little beyond my limited sewing skills.

I recognized how privileged I was to be included in the fantasy, their world, in a fleeting time and space.

So, when the making of the new Star Wars movies was announced, I admit to being excited. Over the years, I had become invested in the characters and their storylines, and I was anxious to see how the next chapters would evolve. Although I didn't see the movie until a few weeks after its release, I was able to avoid spoilers, and so it was a pure experience of fun and wonder. I cheered when original characters appeared on screen for the first time (my apologies to those in the theatre who were not the trusty, and understanding, younger son and friend who accompanied me to the show), came to know and immediately love the new ones, and sat on the edge of my seat during the tense action. In short, I was like a kid again.

I will include no spoilers in this blog. Suffice it to say that I enjoyed every minute of the movie, with the awe of a child, and the freedom of an adult to simply enjoy without worrying about how completely uncool I allowed myself to be. I understand that the next installment will not be out until sometime in 2017. The anticipation of the next adventures for me will be half the fun. In the meantime, I might just have to go back to the theatre to see The Force Awakens again – I suspect it will not be a hard sell to convince my older son to join me once again in the fantasy world that we both loved so much as he was growing up.

January 10, 2016

#FABFEAT: WRITERS' CIRCLE

Writing, by its nature, can be a pretty insular experience. While the final product is shared with others, the process of creation is an individual labour (of love, but hard work nonetheless). For me, the challenge is further heightened by a somewhat (who am I kidding, a fully developed) perfectionist approach to the task. One of the reasons I chose to write via a weekly blog format was because of my tendency to ruminate over my writing, resulting in lots of revisions, but very limited actual output. Being committed to writing and sending out a weekly blog means letting go of my obsessive editing in favour of regularly pressing the publish button. Now more than half way through my 50 Feats, I am much less critical of my work. Where I would have obsessed about typos and other missteps in the past, I can now gratefully accept the occasional email from a friendly reader pointing out a small "oops," edit and update, and…let it go.

My feelings of creative isolation are somewhat mitigated by reader feedback, but I was excited to come across a notice on the Niagara Falls library website advertising a Writers' Circle. My next fabulous feat was confirmed.

Even though I have lived in Niagara Falls for over 25 years, I can count on my one hand the number of times I have visited the Victoria Avenue library site.

I think my older son had a piano recital in one of the community rooms when he was in grade school. I may have accompanied my younger son to a March Break program when he was small. I have a long-expired library card from those days. So, when I walked into the library on the night of the meeting I was impressed by the warm and comfortable atmosphere.

I walked through the various sections looking for the Rosberg Gallery. In my brief travels I saw a familiar face, someone I knew who also struggled with mental health challenges. It had been over a year since we had last crossed paths, and I was so happy to see a big smile spread across his face as he recognized me. He told me he was doing well, involved with a few different projects and loving the experiences. Although our conversation was brief (we both were attending meetings) I was buoyed by another example of a kind and generous soul who had found his way through dark times and learned to live well with mental illness.

I found the little gallery room and joined two other women already seated in chairs that formed part of a circle. I was confident that I was in the right place but confirmed by asking them. After we introduced ourselves, I settled in and glanced around the room at the sketches and paintings on the wall; there were barns and train stations illustrated in charcoal and watercolour displaying varying degrees of experience. Each, however, was displayed without differentiation, respecting talent and the courage to try in equal measures. I really liked this place.

In the next few minutes, several more participants arrived, along with the library group leader. I discovered that the participants had been meeting together on a monthly basis since the previous Fall when the circle began. A more diverse group I could not have imagined: one woman told me she was 89 years old; a man introduced himself as a retired engineer; another woman tentatively told me she was still new to writing, displaying her handwritten pages; a 30-something man greeted the others and settled his iPad on his lap in anticipation; a mother and daughter team rounded out the circle.

Our library leader explained the meeting process for me: each person who wished to receive feedback would read something she or he had written for the group. Some people were writing novels, others poetry, still others wrote passages based upon a topic provided each month as inspiration.

The readings were as varied as the group. Participants shared philosophical dialogues, poetry about Zambonis and cats, a children's adventure story, and the beginnings of a historical novel. Just like the artwork on the walls, some of the writing was stronger than others; again, I respected their courage in opening such personal creations to the world.

When my turn came up, I was nervous. I had the option of listening without sharing, but I felt the need to reciprocate the trust in the room. I explained my premise for 50 Fabulous Feats, and read the first blog feat for the group. When I looked up at the end of my reading, I was greeted with a circle of smiles and encouraging nods. It felt good to have the affirmation of fellow writers.

The hour and a half passed by incredibly quickly. On our way out, I walked with the mother and daughter duo who both said that they hoped to see me again next month. I look forward to it.

March 27, 2016

#FABFEAT: OPEN MIC AT MAHTAY

An exciting part of my 50 Feats adventures has been the ability to discover a variety of events within my own community. One of the main goals in selecting my activities was to support my Niagara community in ways I had not done (or even known about) before I began my blogs. One of my new favourite pastimes is checking out such sites as the St. Catharines Downtown Association (mydowntown.ca) and Niagara Falls Events Calendar where an array of possibilities for the month is presented. The added bonus is that many of the events are free or low cost which makes them more accessible for members of our community.

Several months ago, when I was early for a concert at the new First Ontario Performing Arts Centre in St. Catharines, I dropped into Mahtay Café across the road to pass some time. I was intrigued by the events calendar they had posted on the wall; there were art shows, music, and poetry readings listed, many presented by local talent. I made a note to check out an evening or two. Of course, life happens, and it took me a little while to loop back to this particular feat.

I decided to attend a Thursday night Open Mic to get a sampling of the local talent. I arrived around 7 p.m. for the advertised 7:30 start, found a table and did a little reading while I waited. I wasn't sure what to expect – music, poetry, performance art? The first thing I noticed was that time was relatively fluid for this event as 7:30 turned into 8:30 before anyone actually took to the stage. However, I think I might have been the only one to notice this as people continued to gather, chat, laugh, and generally enjoy the community. As the room filled up, a couple of young men joined my table. While I didn't get their names, we had a long conversation while one waited anxiously for his turn to perform. He had been to Open Mic numerous times before and clearly loved playing guitar and having a venue to do so. In contrast to the young artist were the older men who seemed known to the organizers suggesting they, too, were regulars on this stage. Each had signed up and were called to the stage one by one. The music was varied – some old favourites, some original compositions, folksy to harder rock. There were also differential levels of talent, but the one thing that they all had in common was their pure enjoyment in making music. As someone who can neither sing nor play an instrument, I always appreciate the creation of music by those who both can and do share it with me. I feel their joy and am always buoyed by it.

As I left the café at the end of the evening (or at least the end for me, since I worked the following morning), the friendly hum of the patrons followed me to the door. I stopped to glance at the events calendar on my way out. I saw that one of the upcoming events was a Poetry Slam. There may be more Mahtay evenings for me!

August 2, 2016

#FABFEAT: GETTING "SCHOOLED" AT STREWN

Some people just make me smile. Just thinking about my friend and mentor Pauline has always made me happy – the wonderful memories of working and playing together and the ability to create new experiences with her. Last year, Pauline suggested that we participate in a "Feats with Friends" adventure by going to a cooking class together. As Pauline spends half the year in Mexico, we postponed our feat for her return and last weekend, we travelled to Strewn Winery in Niagara-On-The-Lake for a day at their cooking school.

For anyone who knows me, cooking is not my forte. Okay, that's probably an understatement; my kids would tell you that if it isn't burnt, Mom didn't prepare it. Pauline, on the other hand, is a great cook and she enjoys her time in the kitchen. However, among other traits, Pauline and I share a complete lack of coordination. When we worked together, everyone knew that Pauline was not allowed to have scissor for real and good reasons. Turning us loose on a kitchen with giant knives and multi-bladed food processors was going to be a decidedly exciting time!

We arrived at Strewn early and spent time catching up. A couple joined us a few minutes later and introduced themselves: Wayne and Carol were from

Kincardine and the cooking class had been a gift from Carol's workmates upon her retirement. We easily fell into conversation with this lovely couple. Others began arriving shortly thereafter and we were soon invited into the preparation room where we all received aprons and nametags. Our teacher for the day was Jane who, along with her spouse, Joe, had founded the winery and cooking school twenty years ago. She was bubbly and fun from the get-go and all the students immediately adopted her attitude; I knew immediately that this was going to be a lively day.

After a few opening comments, Jane introduced us to the menu: grilled butterflied pork tenderloin with Niagara fruit salsa; herbed whole wheat couscous; wilted spinach; mixed greens with herb vinaigrette, toasted croutons, tomatoes, and parmesan; poached cherries with wine syrup. We would prepare the meal, and then enjoy it together, paired with Strewn wine. I confess that the menu seemed a little beyond my cooking scope, but I was confident in Pauline's skills. I was also more than pleased when we were instructed to select another pair as our work station partners; of course, we chose the lovely Carol and Wayne.

Our cooking experience was intertwined with friendly conversation, lots of laughs, and, dare I say, even a few cooking tips: using a spoon to peel ginger; the best way to cut a pepper; how best to remove the silver skin from pork tenderloin. With each measure, cut, and stir, the efficient Esther whisked away (pun intended) the used instruments and returned them clean and ready for the next step. We all commented on how much better cooking at home would be if we had our own Esther there.

Lest you think our morning was all work and no play, part way through the class we have a snack break after preparing a lemony lentil spread with mint that was freshly picked. Each group of four prepared their own version and taste-tested the various outcomes on crunchy sweet potato crackers and accompanied by a yummy Strewn wine. Pauline's addition of a little more tahini (which I learned is made of sesame seeds) made our team's spread the definitive winner!

Throughout the class, Jane would gather us together at one of the workstations and demonstrate a technique, then have one of the students replicate her instructions. My turn came when we were pitting cherries (I suspect that Jane chose a relatively danger-free task for me after observing me as I tried to chop ginger earlier in the day). As I pressed the pitting device, the stone flew one way and the cherry arched over my work station and onto the floor; I quickly tossed it into the garbage only to be "schooled" on how a quick rinse was all that was necessary to ensure we made the most of the last cherries of the season.

With most everything prepared, we sat together at a beautifully set table to enjoy our salad with its fresh mixed greens, expertly cut tomatoes (I did that!), and crunchy just-toasted croutons (that was all Pauline). Joe joined us and provided a description of the wine as well as some general pairing principles (such as, the "heavier" the food, the more full-bodied the wine).

With a little more cutting and mixing, we were ready to grill the pork. With the "ding" of the timer, we turned it; with the next ring we plated it, and tented with foil to reabsorb the juices. The only thing left was to make up our plates before we sat together again to enjoy the fruits of our labours. By now the conversation was flowing and we commented on how wonderful the meal and the company was. Outside the glass panels of our dining area, visitors to Strewn peered longingly at our succulent fare. Joe again provided us with information about our wine pairings as well as some history of the winery itself.

We completed our meal with our poached cherries topped with fresh whipped cream. We all commented that this was a meal that we felt we could make at home, albeit without the efficient Esther it would be more of a chore to clean up. Although I confess that Pauline did the lion's share of the work, I did feel just a little like an actual cook at the end of the day.

As we prepared to leave, I gave Wayne and Carol my contact information and promised to share my blog with them. I believe that this feat ranks as one of my favourites – it involved food, friends, fun, and was well and truly fabulous.

August 16, 2016

#FABFEAT: RAILS, BRIDGES, AND BUTCHER SHOPS

In the course of my 50 Feats I have had the pleasure of finding out about interesting and informative events taking place in my own community. This week's activity came to me from the City of Niagara Falls. The description invited me to "join the City's Official Historian, Sherman Zavitz, for a walk into the past as you explore parts of Queen Street, Erie Avenue, Park Street, Zimmerman Avenue, Cataract Avenue, and Bridge Street." I quickly filled out my registration form and looked forward to a Sunday afternoon stroll through Niagara Falls.

The day of the event I arrived for the 1:30 start time. I wasn't sure of the potential interest in the event and, honestly, had envisioned the potential of me and the historian on a personal one-on-one tour. I was pleasantly surprised when I rounded the corner and found about 50 people milling around the stairs of the Queen Street City Hall.

This was a feat that I decided to do solo with a view to meeting some new people while learning about Niagara Falls history. As we waited for the tour to begin, I began talking to Ann. She was carrying a shopping carrier and began to talk to me about Rosbergs and showed me the plastic bags she would distribute as part of the tour. She told me about going to the department store after her music lessons as a girl; she described how old Mrs. Rosbergs acted as elevator operator and kept all the young shoppers in line. What I didn't realize until later was that Ann was Sherman's wife, supporting him in the presentation and throughout the tour.

After a few minutes, Sherman stood at the top of the stairs and began our tour with a description of the Clifton Town Hall that had housed the area's butcher shops. We started a slow stroll towards our next destination and I fell into conversation with a woman who told me she had been a bookkeeper at Rosbergs before it closed. She also shared fond memories of her time at the store. During the presentation, one of the Rosbergs' grandsons who had come specifically for the tour, also contributed to the conversation.

At each stop in the tour, we learned about the various buildings, railroads, shops, and hotels. There was the bank where a famous robbery took place: the culprits rented the building next door and tunneled though to the vault over several weeks at night, taking almost a million dollars back in the early 1900's. They were caught because of a liquor bottle left behind; buying liquor required a recorded name and address upon purchase and the police found the robbers in Montreal, at the very address they had provided. Just as informative were the two older women who giggled as they told me about their experiences with ordering alcohol "back in the day." They said that they had to order food with their alcohol and described the "cardboard sandwiches" that came with their drink order; under no circumstances would they ever touch the sandwiches. We all laughed together as we walked to the next site.

Our next stop was the old post office in Niagara Falls. It's claim-to-fame was its inclusion in the Marilyn Monroe movie Niagara, where she was filmed walking up the stairs. A beautiful old building, it was under some renovations; one woman said that she thought she had seen a person in one of the upper windows – a worker or someone from the past?

We finished our tour by the Niagara Falls bridge. Sherman talked about how the railroad had spanned the United States and Canada. While many of the hotels had closed or burned down over the years, he described the bustling business that had been part of the core of Niagara Falls in its heyday. For me, it was a beautiful reminder of why I am a proud resident of Niagara Falls. One of the participants asked if our guide had written any books about the area and, with a humble smile, Sherman told us there were a few.

When we completed our tour, I made my way back to my car, feeling happy about the people, places, and things I had learned more about during the afternoon. When I got home I found Sherman's book,

Niagara Falls: Historical Notes, with its vignettes about the city and its people. Another successful feat for the history books!

September 25, 2016

#FABFEAT: A NIGHT AT THE MUSEUM

After my adventure at the Niagara Falls Museum, I was excited about having a little more culture with a dash or two of fun this week. My work friend (having passed FabFeats initiation with "flying" colours as my zip line compadre) suggested that we check out the final night of Open Late at the St. Catharines Museum and Welland Canal Centre. The advertisement promised food, music, and the opportunity to participate in "audience-led museum tours as co-curators" for the reasonable price of five dollars.

Our evening began on a comical note as I waited patiently on a bench outside for her to arrive, only to discover some time later through our texting that she had entered through a side door and was already inside, thinking I had been held up in getting there. Fortunately, almost as soon as we met, they were announcing the first "Museum Secrets" tour was about to begin.

We found ourselves among a small group of women gathered around a young tour guide named Adrian. He was just about to start when I recognized one of the participants as someone I used to work with at my last job. We had a mini-reunion while the tour guide waited patiently. He then began to explain our awaiting adventure. The tour would consist of five items, each with two distinct descriptions, one of which was the truth, and one a ruse. Our task was to determine the correct story. Adrian told us that we could not ask him any questions (or at least, that if we did, he would provide no answers) and there was no touching any of the objects. With this segue, he noted that one of our group members had located the first mystery item by resting her purse on it while she took off her coat. With a little laugh, and a touch of embarrassment, she withdrew her purse and Adrian asked who might like to read the first description. My friend stepped up immediately and told us that the big yellow metal object was, in fact, a buoy that had been in the waters of the canal. Or was it? The next story told of a war time air raid siren. We looked closely at (but didn't touch) the item for clues as to its actual origin. Someone commented on the black hose at the bottom; another suggested the heavy metal did not look very buoyant. Adrian just smiled and lead us to the next mystery item.

For the next 30 minutes we weaved our way through the museum, studying an early 1900's picture (does it depict rum runners or canal workers?), a wooden cone that opened into tiny parts (a model of volume or the conical portion of an eye?), a pair of glasses (to whom did they belong?), and a travelling chest (while it turned out _not_ to belong to an unlucky seafarer who was on board not one, not two, but three vessels that ended in tragedy – including the Titanic – Adrian told us that the story itself was true). During our travels, we developed a kind of camaraderie as we shared our thoughts and had a few laughs along the way. As we came to the final stop, Adrian recapped our items and possible provenance. The group then chose based on our best sleuthing skills; most us correctly answered four of the five, with only one woman not tripped up by the sneaky positioning of the glasses beside the Lightening Fastener exhibit causing us to wrongly select Gideon Sundback as their owner. Before we departed, Adrian had us all raise our right hands and swear to maintain the "mysteries" of the evening and reveal nothing to future participants.

Next up was dinner. A food truck sat out front advertising its British fare; Ello Gov'na promised "smashing good nosh" including bangers and mash that my friend decided upon and a roast beef in Yorkshire pudding sandwich that called out to me. We took our yummy food to the back of the museum and chatted while we watched a ship travel through the canal as the sun began to set.

As the evening cooled off, we made our way inside to await the evening's musical entertainment: Beth Moore Music. We spent some time wandering around the various exhibits and had a little laugh each time we heard Adrian taking his next group around for their "mystery tour," feeling a little smug about knowing the answers, but staying true to our oath of secrecy. By the time Beth took the stage, it was past 8:30 and I admit to feeling just a bit old as

I calculated how late I could stay and still get the requisite sleep needed to fire on all cylinders the next day at work. She began with a couple of songs on her own, before being joined by two young men on percussion and keyboards. They were very good, and I noted that it was too bad there were not more people in attendance. I particularly enjoyed Beth's explanations of the background to her various lyrics; for me, it really is all about the story. Reluctantly, my friend and I slipped away after a few more songs to make our way home before too late an hour (which, I might add, is definitely different at 51 than it was at 21!).

As I drove home I realized that this event marked my 48th Fabulous Feat. Stay tuned for the next couple, my SilverLiningFrog friends, as they promise to dazzle and delight.

October 12, 2016

PILLAR OF POSITIVITY #5:
Developing Coping Strategies

Everyone experiences stress, adversity, and heartache in life – it is just a part of being human. Some people live with more difficulties and it is true that those challenged with mental illness are especially impacted by the stressors of everyday life. Nonetheless, we can all support our own mental health by developing effective and positive coping strategies that allow us not just to survive, but thrive.

According to Sonja Lyubomirsky, "coping is what people do to alleviate the hurt, stress, or suffering caused by a negative event or situation." In her book, *The How of Happiness*, Dr. Lyubomirsky describes two types of coping: problem-focused, and emotion-focused. One strategy is not superior to the other, but, while problem-focused takes an analytical, logical "fix it" approach, emotion-focused recognizes that not everything is managed through a concrete list of steps. For example, when a loved one dies, emotion-focused strategies such as talking to a friend and remembering the positives of the relationship in the face of the loss can facilitate acceptance and even support post-traumatic growth and transformation.

I appreciate the challenge of developing coping positive strategies. I have enlisted more than my fair share of negative approaches, including self-medicating with alcohol, when faced with what felt like overwhelming situations. I now know that my ability to develop and use solid coping practices has allowed me to become more resilient to the difficulties that life inevitably presents me. Over time, I have experienced the benefits of building my positive coping muscles including better physical health, reduced stress, and the meaning a purpose that comes from sharing this information with others; research also supports the gains experienced by those who implement positive ways of dealing with life's difficulties.

There is no shortage of examples of positive coping practices. Below are just a few that you might like to try:

- Take a hot bath
- Listening to your favourite music and, maybe, singing and dancing to it
- Writing about your thoughts in a journal
- Going for a walk, run, or bike ride outside
- Calling a friend
- Listening to a guided meditation
- Engaging in some deep breathing
- Taking a nap
- Practicing an act of kindness for a stranger
- Having a cup of tea
- Reading a book
- Watching an uplifting movie

- Doing some gardening
- Going to a yoga class
- Eating a healthy meal
- Getting a massage

"Problems are not the problem; coping is the problem." – Virginia Satir

April 10, 2017

#FABEATS: MIND OVER MAKEOVER

This activity may not be much of an achievement for most, but, for me, it is both a feat and a first. I have always been a little uncomfortable with things that might be self-indulgent – probably my Scottish Presbyterian roots – but my avoidance of such things as makeovers, massages, and the like wasn't really about extravagance; my anxiety was the true reason for turning down these opportunities in the past.

Many people deal with claustrophobia, but my anxiety ran just a little deeper. Since childhood, I have dealt with enormous fear when anyone enters my personal space, particularly around my face. I was equally as white knuckled gripping the chair in the hair salon as I was at the dentist. I would have to focus all my energy to stay seated, to minimize the trembling, to not simply get up and run. The anxiety was worse than any physical hurt could have been (although, I am pretty sure from what I can remember that childbirth was no picnic either). When other people spoke of the fun of getting a facial or having their makeup professionally done, I dismissed it as "just not my thing," but the truth is that, for me, it would have been more torturous than luxurious.

I thought that I was the only person who dealt with such an odd anxiety, but, recently, I discovered some research related to peripersonal space (that is the scientific term for the space around our bodies that people consider to be psychologically theirs) and anxiety. Not surprisingly, those individuals who live with anxiety have larger peripersonal spaces than those who do not, especially for the high-risk area around the face. For those with higher anxiety, threats were perceived as closer than was the case for non-anxious subjects, despite the stimuli being the same distance away; anxious individuals had a larger defensive peripersonal space. Maybe I wasn't the only person sweating it out at the hair salon after all.

As an adult, I have dealt with my anxiety through both medical (I take medication for depression and anxiety) and nonmedical means (I have learned anxiety-reducing strategies such as breathing techniques, visualization and meditation). I still get the occasional tremor when I am sitting in the hairstylist's chair, but I also find myself able to somewhat enjoy the experience.

So, when I was putting together my list of feats, I decided that I would include one that would celebrate my ability to manage my defensive peripersonal space by having a professional makeup lesson. What better time to get tips for looking my best as I step over that half century line.

Accompanied by my dear friend Liz, I tentatively approached the reception desk of a local salon and signed up for a little self-indulgence. For over an hour, I let the lovely Adriana pamper me. Not only did I have my makeup done, I had my eyebrows shaped and a mini-facial. Whew!

I am happy to report I only had a couple of moments of anxiety – and that was mostly because my "smoky eyes" made me look more surprised than sultry, suggesting Nora Desmond rather than Gisele Bündchen (I'm ready for my close-up Mr. DeMille).

The verdict on this feat: interesting to try, and, though not likely to be a regular thing for me, a definite triumph. Now, if I could just learn to relax at the dentist…

September 9, 2015

#FABEAT: THE OTHER SIDE OF THE TABLE

It has been over 25 years since I have had a job interview. I was one of the fortunate people who was hired right out of university into an organization and profession I was able to enjoy for over a quarter century. One of my main functions for many of those years was recruitment; it was also one of my favourite portfolios. I loved the opportunity to match talented individuals with just the right position. I always tried to make committee interviews as comfortable as possible, so each person could demonstrate his or her best self and determine if this job was the right fit from their perspective as well as ours.

I consider myself a very seasoned interviewer; however, I can't say the same about my experience as an interviewee. While I had the opportunity to work in different areas of Human Resources during my career, I evolved into those roles without ever having to be on the other side of the table in an interview situation. During the last year and a half, I have been focused full-time on completing my M.Ed. and so it has only been in the last few months, as I finish my final course, that the prospect of being an interviewee entered my thoughts.

Engaging in a job search after such a long time in one career at one organization has been a new challenge. Some days I am filled with the excitement of all the possibilities; others I wonder whether my age is an advantage or a drawback. Fortunately, I have had the opportunity to work with a wonderful job coach who has helped me to discover the type of work that gives me energy by playing to my strengths and passions. This exploration has allowed me to consider work that is outside what I would have previously considered myself qualified to undertake.

However, all this preparation did not make me any less nervous as I readied for my very first interview. While I am generally a confident and outgoing person, I worried about how I would perform in the hot seat. Despite my years of experience in recruitment, I turned to the internet to see what the latest articles suggested regarding how to prepare for an interview. Interestingly, google completed my search with "how to prepare for an… earthquake"; I'm assuming both are equally as nerve-wracking.

Not surprisingly, the information contained in the various commentaries were mostly not new to me: research the organization; anticipate potential questions; review your resume; plan what to wear… Yikes, for the better part of the last 18 months I had lived in my jeans-and-tshirt student uniform. Fortunately for me, previously-working Susan had the foresight to buy suit pants with an elastic-waist that still fit present-day larger-sized Susan, saving me the agony of having to go shopping.

On the day of the interview, I arrived early, and waited in the reception area. Understandably anxious, I decided to use information from a TedTalk by Amy Cuddy to enhance my confidence with a two-minute power pose while I waited. I used the "Wonder Woman" which has been shown to increase testosterone and decrease cortisol in stressful situations. I tried to disguise my posture by looking at the decorations on the wall as I stood feet apart, hands on my hips, not wanting to be "caught" in the moment.

The interview itself, I am relieved to say, was a very positive experience. The panel was friendly, and we engaged in a conversation rather than The Spanish Inquisition that I had feared. I left the meeting feeling like I had been able to present my best self. As well, I felt I had learned enough about the organization to know I would be comfortable in the environment should I be selected for the job.

In the end, another candidate was selected for this position. While I was disappointed, I did not have any regrets about the experience. I was thankful to have had such a positive return to the world of interviews, and confident that I will find the right opportunity for me in the not-too-distant future.

For those of you who may also be engaging in a job search, I wanted to give you a few tips that I didn't find in the hundreds of articles on how to prepare for an interview:

- Take the time to discover who you are and what you love before you strike out on your job search; we spend a lot of our lives at work and we are both happiest and most productive when we can play to our strengths and do something that gives us meaning and purpose.
- Think about not just what you have done before, but the transferable nature of your skills and experiences from all areas of your life: work, home, and community activities all count.
- Remember that the interview is a two-way dialogue and that you want to learn enough to assess whether the job is a fit for you as much as the interviewers want to make their determinations.
- Be your authentic self in the interview; the person who is hired is the person who needs to show up every day to work and, while it may be easy to put on a different persona for an hour, it is draining to have to put on that mask every day to go to work.
- Let it go; second guessing your answers and beating yourself up about what you did or did not say after an interview is a recipe for unhappiness so, instead, give yourself credit for having the courage to put yourself out there and celebrate this accomplishment.
- Finally, check out social psychologist Amy Cuddy's TedTalk about the impact of power

poses - it costs absolutely nothing to try it and it may just help you get over the jitters and present your best self!

November 14, 2015

#FABFEAT: BEING BRAVE FOR BRENÉ

This week's feat falls under the category of "fun with a purpose." I was particularly interested in participating in this experience because it was inspired by the work of Dr. Brené Brown, who is a hero of mine. Dr. Brown, who describes herself as a researcher/storyteller, explains her qualitative research by declaring "stories are just data with a soul." One of the volunteers from the Canadian Mental Health Association – Niagara Branch recently read *Daring Greatly* and decided to try out the core value of courage through vulnerability and invited others to join her in "showing up and letting ourselves be seen."

The plan was for a few kindred spirits to band together in a flash mob. In this case, we wouldn't be wearing our hearts on our sleeves; our messages would be written on our shirts. The idea was to write a personal insecurity that we have some discomfort sharing on the front of the shirt and an accepting statement that contradicted it on the back. We would all meet at a certain place and time, throw off our coats to reveal our shirts of vulnerability, and perform a dance routine to Sara Bareilles, *Brave*.

In case you were wondering why on earth we would want to do this, Dr. Brown's research has supported the need to embrace our vulnerability to truly experience joy, love, belonging and connection. Our flash mob leader in this feat wrote the following: "To be accepted as you are, without judgement, is a very powerful feeling. Hopefully this event will empower each of us as we encourage others to be Brave too."

I was enthusiastic about the event, but a little intimidated by the choreographed routine part given my less-than-coordinated dance skills. Nonetheless, I jumped in with both (left) feet. Having not been able to attend the first rehearsal, my first glimpse of the group practice was on a video sent so we could teach ourselves the moves. The dance began with two very talented dance teachers engaged in (from my perspective) wildly complicated steps and gestures, followed by some kids from a dance group who were part of the troupe. At the first chorus, the rest of the "mob" joined in.

My first instinct upon seeing the video was to come down with a contagious illness from which I would not recover until after the flash mob performance. But, I chose instead to "dare greatly" and I attended the next rehearsal where a very patient instructor broke down the moves for me and a couple of other neophytes to the point that I was only one or two steps behind everyone else at the end of the hour. We had one more dress rehearsal the day before the event. By then I had decided that I would be less concerned about delivering a perfect performance and more tuned into having fun with the whole experience.

We met up at the mall and learned our mob would take over the food court where, hopefully, we would have an audience of Christmas shoppers. Speakers and cameras were set up as unobtrusively as possible, and then the music started. Just as in the rehearsals, the instructors began their beautiful routine, joined first by the kids, and, finally, by the rest of us. I managed to mostly stay with the group, and, more importantly, I thoroughly enjoyed myself, absorbing the positive energy from those around me. In our final move, we all turned our backs to face the crowd, pointing at our statements of strength. My shirt said, "I am afraid to show the REAL ME" on the front, and "But I will DARE GREATLY and let my light shine" on the back. As I pointed my thumbs at the words, I felt a rush of adrenaline; it is my hope that our feat might inspire other to cast off the shadows of fear, and bravely let your beautiful, imperfect, lovely lights shine.

November 29, 2015

#FABEAT: FUN ON THE HILL

For people who live in Niagara Falls, Clifton Hill is a place visited only when visitors come and want the whole Falls experience; otherwise, we generally avoid the crowds and traffic as much as is possible. That was, of course, before I took on my 50 Fabulous Feats adventure.

Every year in January, the awesome attractions on The Hill participate in a charity day in support of Cystic Fibrosis research. This is the 28th year that certain activities can be enjoyed by local residents for only a loonie. This year, when I saw a posting online advertising the day, I decided to get in on the fun. I enlisted my older son as my companion for the day (his younger brother was too overwhelmed with course assignments to accompany us – at least, that was his story).

I confess that I may have also had to offer a Falls Manor breakfast as incentive to get my son on board. We were on the road to the Falls by 10:30 as I wasn't sure what the crowds would be like. The weather fluctuated between drizzly and downright pouring rain, so I felt confident that few people would be making the trek. I was wrong.

We turned into one of the large public parking lots on Clifton Hill and joined the line of locals who also chose to brave the elements for some cheap fun.

When I gathered up my umbrella, I discovered it was only half functional, but it was enough to fend off most of the rain.

There were already long lines forming at the various attractions. Fortunately for us, I get sick on any kind of 3D ride, so we didn't head in the direction of those popular rides. Instead, I had my heart set on the Movieland Wax Museum. Thankfully, the line was short, and my son, lulled into a French Toast coma, didn't balk at my choice.

Within a couple of minutes, we were to the front of the line and exchanged a toonie for tickets for both of us. It was as silly as I had anticipated with wax figures of everyone from Clint Eastwood to ET, Cary Grant to Jim Carrey. We walked through the winding aisles and giggled like kids as we took pictures with "the stars" – I even got to hug Homer and sit on the couch with the Simpson family.

After we came out of the wax museum, the rain was still coming down, and the crowds started to cause a little anxiety for my son; we solved both concerns by going into the building that housed Boston Pizza and the dazzling Rock 'n Roll Bowling Alley. Although bowling wasn't part of the dollar days, we were the only patrons and decided this was our next adventure. As a kid, I fondly remember my cousin Anne and I used to regularly go to the downtown Brampton bowling alley, but it had been a long time since I had thrown a bowling ball (yes, thrown is the accurate word when it comes to my bowling prowess).

We rented our stylish shoes, and I picked the lightest ball I could find (which still felt ridiculously heavy) and let the games begin. I admit to smittenly trash-talking upon my first strike, but soon was humbled by throwing at least as many gutter balls as those that hit any pins – inconsistent would be the appropriate characterization of my game. Nonetheless, I still gloated about my 2-point win.

When we returned to the street, the crowds had increased, and we mutually decided that lunch rather than another attraction was our preferred course of action. While we ate our food, I watched the array of people walking up and down The Hill. There were families with small children awed by the experience, couples hand-in-hand gazing lovingly at each other, groups of teenaged boys trying to look cool, and packs of teenaged girls trying rather unsuccessfully to ignore the teenaged boys. They all made me smile and realize that Clifton Hill was pure fun no matter your age.

As we returned to our car, I stopped at a one of the dinosaur displays to strike a pose, defective umbrella at half-mast as if it had battled the giant lizards à la Jurassic Park. Another feat accomplished, another novel experience under my belt.

January 18, 2017

#FABFEAT: ADVENTURES IN HOSPITAL-LAND

For those who follow my blog, you might be scratching your head a little by the title of this feat. In my last post, my upcoming activity was listed as "a little live history at the Niagara Falls Battleground Museum." However, as happens in life, the Universe decided that this week's adventure would involve an entirely different kind of event.

On Saturday, I purchased my tickets, and was spending time with my older son trying to cajole him into coming with me on Sunday, both for company and as a potential way to lift his mood a bit. He lives with bipolar disorder, generalized anxiety disorder, and panic disorder and, while he lives well despite some of the limitations of his illness, there are times when his fluctuating moods, particularly the depression, can be difficult. In the previous month he had been very energetic, even working extra hours at his part-time job. However, as is often the case, it is likely that this burst of vigor signaled a hypomania that is typical of his Bipolar II. Over the last couple of weeks, he had been experiencing the down side that often follows these episodes of elevated mood – sleeping up to 18 hours a day, high anxiety, depressed mood.

I received a phone call from him around 11 p.m. on Saturday night. He and his Dad were on the way to the hospital; the fear of hurting himself had surpassed his dread of hospitals. I met them in the emergency waiting area and thus began our adventure in hospital-land. I describe it as such not to make light of a serious situation, but as a coping strategy that both my son and I use frequently when we are dealing with anxiety – good old, sometimes incongruous, humour. As we were in Niagara Falls, and the mental health facilities for the Region are now housed in St. Catharines, we were placed into the hospital wheel of acronyms to access PERT on the OTN (Psychiatric Emergency Response Team over the Ontario Telehealth Network video conferencing). It was a busy Saturday night, and it would be 3 a.m. before the PERT Nurse was able to contact us. The emergency nurses kindly gave my son a bed so that he could sleep a little while awaiting the call.

During the phone conference, my son expressed his ongoing fear of being left alone because of his suicidal thoughts. He then was given several options including access Safe Beds. where he would receive therapeutic support in a protected environment, or awaiting a consult with a psychiatrist. After a short discussion, he decided to talk to the psychiatrist. Unfortunately, it would be 8 a.m. before a psychiatrist was on shift in St. Catharines. The lovely nurses in Niagara Falls set us up in a room, and brought in a reclining lounge chair so I could stay with him until the psychiatrist was available via OTN.

We were fortunately tired enough that we both slept on and off until the psychiatrist was available around 10 a.m. He was attentive to my son's distress and suggested that given his state, and the fact that he did not have any psychiatric services working with him currently (he has been on the wait list to return to the Mood Disorders Clinic for over a year), it might be helpful to be admitted to hospital for a few days. My son had always described admittance as one of his worst nightmares, but, to his credit, he was insightful enough to know that he needed something to change for him to remain safe and become well again.

Several hours later he was transferred via ambulance to the St. Catharines site to access the Mental Health Unit. While his admission was voluntary, it didn't change the fact that he was now in a facility that restricted his ability to come and go. Being on the inside of a locked unit is a scary feeling for anyone; for someone who struggles with severe anxiety, the discomfort can increase exponentially. As a mother, I felt moments of helplessness when his fears were especially heightened. But, we knew we were in the right place for him to get the professional support he needed. I tried to lessen his fears by looking at the positive side of things. However, he sometimes articulated his need to just be in the negativity; it didn't matter how nice the room was or how pleasant and supportive the staff were when I finally had to leave him for the night.

You may be asking yourself, how does this experience qualify as a "fabulous feat?" It is definitely a novel, intentional activity, but where's the positivity and the fun? Despite the challenges of the last week, the upsides of this adventure are significant. We know that my son is in the best place, with experts who can support him through medication and counselling to return to a place of wellness. My son has shown to himself and others the incredible resilience he is capable of through the sheer act of voluntarily admission. As well, he continues to fight against the stigma associated with mental illness by his willingness to be open about his situation; he posted on his Facebook page that he was in hospital and was very clear that there was no shame in needing support for his mental health challenges. Despite being in hospital, we continue to share small moments of laughter and love each day. Finally, I make a point to be mindful of the positive things around me: the lovely aroma of the peonies on my walk in from the parking lot; stopping for a quick second to enjoy the feel of the sunshine on my face; a bit of "fuzz therapy" from my dogs when I get home after a long day.

As I write this we are on our way out for a day pass. He is progressing well – gaining some coping skills from groups, meeting with and learning from other young people who are experiencing similar difficulties with anxiety and depression, and benefiting from adjustments to his medications through his access to a hospital psychiatrist. I am confident that the process of recovery will continue for all of us, enhanced by the experiences that could only have been acquired by an adventure in hospital-land.

June 5, 2016

#FABFEAT: BECOMING A SPARKIE: PART 1 THE JOURNEY

I am often struck by how life has unfolded around me over the last few years, particularly since I began to implement my own positive psychology practices. I mentioned in my last blog about the personal impact of Barbara Fredrickson's Broaden and Build Theory as I have found myself slowly stretching my previous boundaries by engaging in wondrous adventures that serve to break down the constraints my anxiety has walled around me over the years.

In 2008, having just "come out" about living with mental illness, I decided to put my name forward as a "face" for the Canadian Alliance on Mental Illness and Mental Health Faces of Mental Illness Campaign. I was thrilled to be selected among the participants that year and excited to be invited to the celebrations in Ottawa for Mental Health Awareness Week. As the date came closer, however, my anxiety about travelling alone to Ottawa became too much; I reluctantly declined to attend, using the excuse that I could not take time off work. I felt embarrassed and deflated by the fact that something that was an everyday occurrence for so many others caused such panic in me that I was incapacitated simply by the thought of travelling alone. My thoughts returned again and again to how ridiculously weak I was. The excitement I had felt was replaced by self-flagellation.

Fast forward to 2016: I was reading The Mental Health Commission of Canada online newsletter and saw the call for applications for a training workshop called SPARK – Supporting the Promotion of Activated Research and Knowledge. The program is designed to "help participants apply techniques for moving evidence-informed research and knowledge in mental health, substance use, and addictions more quickly into practice." It sounded like a great match for my 50 Fabulous Feats experiment. It was the last day applications were being accepted, so I put together a brief outline of the SilverLiningFrog concept, the positive psychology research, and my blogs where I shared my own novel, intentional activities in support of improving my mental health and encouraging others to do so.

In early April, I received an email that advised my application had been placed on the waiting list for SPARK participation. Later in the month, I was excited to learn that I was being invited to attend training in Ottawa in June. There was a slight challenge for me to manage as between the time of my application and my acceptance, I had started working at Niagara Region Mental Health. I am forever grateful to both my Manager who allowed me the time off despite being less than two months on the job, and my team members who let me pick up a weekend shift so that I only had to take one day without pay.

The only hurtle left for me was travelling to Ottawa. A lovely MHCC staff member, Hannah, made arrangements to get me there and home again in time for my Friday morning shift. The fastest route available other than driving was a bus, Go Train and a Via Rail train; my old friend, anxiety, reared up at this point. Fortunately, over the last few years I have become more aware when anxiety tries to make decisions for me, and I, in turn, have changed my response from self-judgment, embarrassment, and raging against it, to a more open, self-compassionate mindset.

Kristen Neff, leading researcher in the field of self-compassion, identifies three elements of self-compassion: self-kindness, common humanity, and mindfulness. In its simplest terms, self-compassion involves treating yourself with the same kindness and care we would give to a good friend, recognizing that no one is perfect. Instead of raging against my anxiety, I have learnt to be more aware of it. I have reframed the "negative" aspect by recognizing that the fear is grounded in a desire to keep me safe; I actually have a little conversation with my anxiety expressing gratitude for its underlying protective nature, and walk through the steps I will take to make sure I can and will be okay. It may sound a bit hokey, but making friends with my fears frees up my energy for more productive problem solving.

As the day arrived for my departure for SPARK, I was fully prepared with my tickets carefully tucked in my backpack, taxi pre-arranged to take me to the bus terminal in Niagara Falls, and a mental toolkit of breathing techniques and other grounding exercises should I need them. I began my adventure at 6:30 a.m. moving from taxi to bus to Go train, then onto the Via Rail train that would deliver me to Ottawa just after 3 p.m. I was surprised by how little anxiety I felt. As I transitioned between Go Train and Via Rail at Union Station in Toronto, I became a bit confused. I stopped, took three mindful breaths, and asked some friendly looking young women how I might find Via Rail; not only did they give me directions, they went out of their way to walk me there and we had a lovely conversation on the way. When I sought confirmation from another young woman that she, too, was awaiting the train to Ottawa, she let out a sigh of relief and told me she thought it was, but was glad to hear that I was also travelling that way. With a great deal of what Kristen Neff would call "common humanity," we enjoyed a nice chat before the train arrived and we each departed for our assigned seats. By the time I entered the taxi that took me to my hotel, I was both tired and exhilarated as I had accomplished the first phase of my "fabulous feat" and anticipated the amazing training opportunity that would now bring me together with participants from across Canada with whom I would become an official SPARKie.

July 13, 2016

#FABFEAT: EMPTYING THE NEST

When my younger son came home one day last spring and told me he was applying for an exchange program for his third year of university, I thought perhaps he would go to England or Australia. When I asked about his choices, he told me the best biotechnology program was at Yonsei University in Seoul, South Korea. True to his quiet yet determined spirit, several months later he announced he had been accepted and would be leaving for ten months beginning in late August.

At the time, it seemed like a long way away, but this past week his Dad, my older son and I drove to the Toronto airport and hugged him goodbye as he left for his overseas adventure. There were, of course, a few tears; his were mostly related to having to leave the dogs behind. I had a few emotional moments leading up to his departure, and as we watched him disappear into the airport crowds. I was joyful for his opportunity, but recognized that for the first time ever, the only other cohabitants in my house had four legs and furry coats. While I realized Mike was away for less than a year, it heralded the beginning of the next phase of life for me; the "nest" was emptying.

Other than one year almost 30 years ago when I began my first job and moved to Niagara, I have never lived alone. I have spent time alone, and am quite comfortable with my own company, but there was always someone I could expect to arrive home, if only for a rest (believe me when I say that neither of my boys were ever lured home by the promise of their Mom's cooking, unless it had been prepared in advance by Mr. Zehr). The coming year would see me as the sole human resident at Casa Mifsud.

As I regarded my surroundings in this new light, I became inspired. After ten years living in my house, I had brought, bought, and acquired a mishmash of stuff. Closets bulge with unworn items, storage spaces hold boxes unopened since arriving, rooms display items that produce more clutter than joy. The empty nest could be the impetus for an emptying of the nest.

The week since Mike's departure was a busy one for me, without a great deal of time to think about next steps. Friday night saw me out with friends on the patio of a local restaurant where we all talked about the various life changes that we were experiencing. As the sun set, we noticed a tiny frog (it might have been a toad) slowly hopping his way past our table. It would seem that my spirit animal was approving of my next life transformation. Let the emptying begin.

August 30, 2016

First feat: A motorcycle ride on my birthday

Graduating with my M.Ed.

Me and My 2 Most Fabulous Feats

Sushi for Susan

Feats with a friend: Just horsin' around

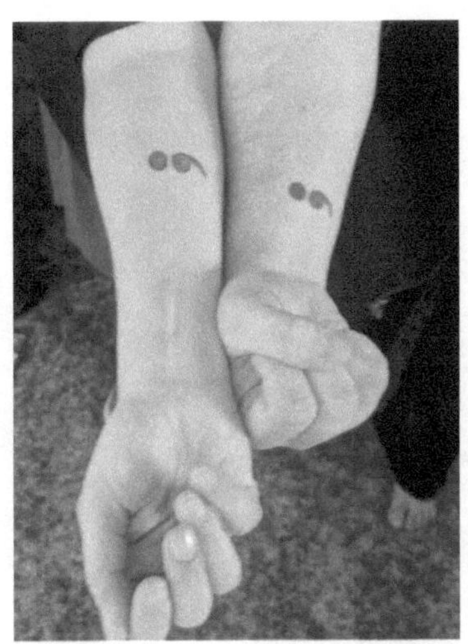

Sharing our semi-colons

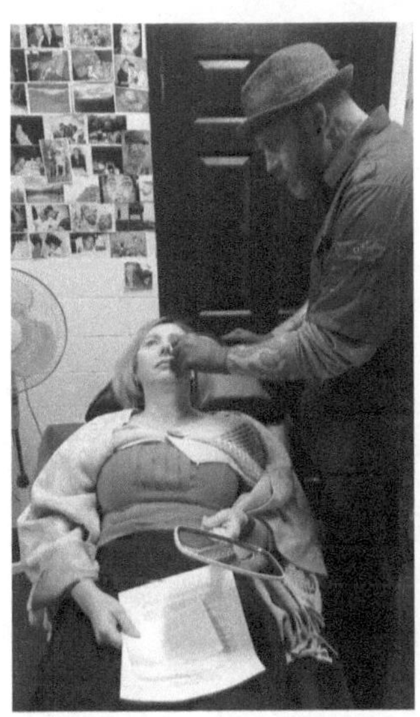

To pierce or not to pierce; question answered

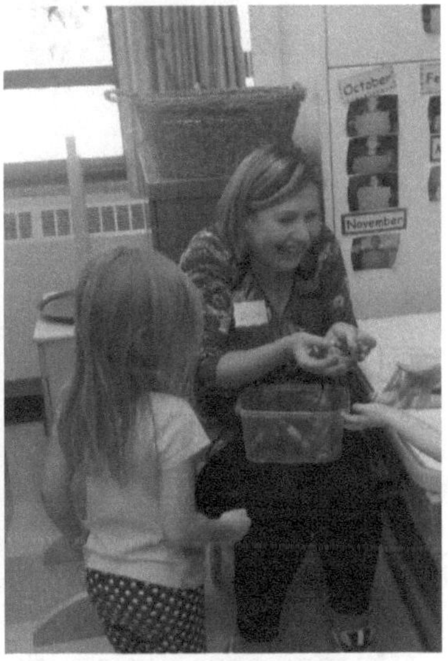

Scientist Sue and the coveted octopus

A day at the museum

Blood donor clinic with helpful volunteer Janet

A fish "tale" from Kauai

A bit of fun on Clifton Hill

PILLAR OF POSITIVITY #6:
Savouring Life's Joys

I have always been a "glass half-full" kind of person, despite my struggle with depression and anxiety. However, I often missed out on the fleeting moment of joy because of anxiety about some potential future disaster or ruminations about how I might have better dealt with situations that had already taken place. When I was introduced to the concept of savouring, I almost dismissed it as being too simplistic to make any sort of difference in my life. Stopping to smell the roses seemed a little clichéd and surely couldn't make an impact on my daily challenges. Yet, as I read about the related research, I came to the realization that the ability to appreciate the good things in life – big and small – was one of the most effective strategies for improving depression and reducing stress.

Barbara Fredrickson, one of my positive psychology researcher rock stars, defines savouring as "considering good events in such a way that you willfully generate, intensify, and prolong your heartfelt enjoyment of them." Researcher Fred Bryant describes how savouring is not just about the present moment, but has a past and a future element. Think about an outing with friends: you can benefit from planning where you will go and what you will do; you gain enjoyment in the moment; and later, you can savour the memory of the time you spent together.

Savouring can also transform routine experiences into small moments of delight. Having eaten more than my fair share of meals while mindlessly watching TV or thinking about what I needed to get done that day, I decided to try a few practices that focused on mindfully eating, using all my senses to appreciate something as small as a raisin. Instead of driving to work in autopilot, I purposefully looked at blossoms on the trees and the little dog in the car stopped next to me at a red light as he enjoyed the sights and smells of the world from his open window.

I found that I could insert these moments of savouring into my day even when – especially when – there were significant challenges in my life. I remember when my son was in hospital in the mental health unit and I would visit him in the morning before work. Each day I would stop at the front of the entrance where beautiful pink flowers were blooming. I would close my eyes and breathe in their sweet scent; sometimes I would touch the velvety petals before I made my way inside.

Perhaps the most special part of my adoption of savouring practices was the joy I found in the shared experiences I had with others during my 50 feats and the ability to mutually reminisce which increased the happiness quotient for all of us. Whether it was eating sushi, getting my nose pierced, or flying through the sky on the Niagara Falls zip line, being able to talk about the fun of it all with those great friends and family who were along for the ride brings fresh positivity and a spark of energy to plan a new adventure.

I discovered that the practice of savouring was absolutely beautiful in its simplicity. In addition to the examples I have described, below are a few more ideas for your own savouring practice:

- Use your camera to really notice and preserve the beauty in the world around you.
- Create a savouring album or box that contains meaningful pictures or items and regularly look at it and think about the joy of each piece.
- Have an adventure with a friend – plan the details, enjoy the moment, reconnect later to remember the fun.
- Eat a meal without any distractions – use all of your senses to appreciate each bite.
- Go to an art gallery and experience the awe of its contents.

- And, of course, take a mindful walk – stop and smell the roses.

"Savor the moments that are warm and special and giggly" – Sammy Davis Jr.

May 1, 2017

#FABFEAT: LIFE IN THE FAST LANE

How fortunate I was to be able to start my 50 feats by taking my very first motorcycle ride! Mother Nature was kind to me and provided a beautiful, sunny day for my adventure and the Universe arranged for a wonderful friend and his gorgeous, red motorcycle to be available to take me on my actual birthday.

I had a little learning to do in advance of the trip: what to wear – long pants, boots, a jacket, helmet, of course; what to do – get on and off from the left, keep your feet up at stops; what not to do – leaning in the opposite direction to the driver when turning can dump the bike.

With the basics covered, we were on our way. I was tentative at first; holding on for dear life probably best describes my riding style. But, it wasn't long before I was able to just experience the thrill of feeling the wind in my face (a little bonus – a temporary face lift and exfoliation from the force of the air combined with the occasional bug), and the rush of speeding along with only the motorcycle between me and the great everything.

While I was merely a passenger, I can totally understand the appeal of driving a motorcycle. A 2013 study by Kelton (http://keltonglobal.com/in-the-media/harley-davidson-study-women-who-ride-are-happier-more-fulfilled/), commissioned by Harley Davidson, found that female riders reported feeling more confident and satisfied with their appearance than non-riders. As well, more than half described themselves as feeling happier and almost 75% believed their lives had improved since they started riding. Perhaps that is part of the communion between drivers who, when passing each other on the road, give a little wave, a low-handed peace sign, a motorcycle equivalent of 'namaste' – the rider spirit in me acknowledges the rider spirit in you.

Even as a passenger, I felt an incredible freedom in being so close to world around me, the wild adrenaline spike zooming up and down hills, and being seemingly suspended in mid-air as we leaned towards the ground around curves. I confess to engaging in several bouts of uncool whooping and hollering with glee like a child on an amusement park ride.

When I chose my feat, it was not to *drive* a motorcycle (breathe easy all who are familiar with my driving prowess). I wanted to be a passenger, which I think also provided a unique and powerful perspective. While the motorcycle drivers in the Kelton study expressed a feeling of independence, I enjoyed the trust relationship that is part of the passenger-driver connection. As I have noted in previous posts, I live with anxiety and am generally not much of a risk taker. In *The Geography of Bliss,* Eric Weiner suggests trust is necessary for happiness and that both trusting and being trusted are significant factors in having a blissful life. I discovered that the same is true of having a successful motorcycle ride: I had complete faith in the skills of my driver, and knew he would keep me safe; in turn, he trusted that I would follow his lead, remembering the do's and don'ts, and just enjoy the ride. So simple, but impossible to achieve without solid faith in each other. And not lost on me as a metaphor for life.

How blessed I have been to begin my journey of fabulous feats with such a magnificent experience! My thanks go out to Mother Nature, and my great friend Les for an adventure to reflect upon and remember.

July 23, 2015

#FABFEAT: SUSHI FOR SUSAN

Anyone familiar with my family growing up would likely know that fish wasn't often on the menu. My Mom was not, in her words, "a fish person." She didn't like the smell of fish, especially the aroma that fills the house when it is cooking. The closest we came to fish dinners were Hunt's fish and chips on a special Friday night (the battered halibut and crunchy fries arrived wrapped in newspaper) and the odd breakfast bass or perch fillet fried up at the cottage freshly caught that day from the Georgian Bay. And, after joining Weight Watchers when she was just about my age and middle-aged spread was becoming a challenge, solid white tuna in water also made its way into our meals.

Because of my limited exposure to fish as a child, and potentially exacerbated by inheriting my Mom's taste buds, I have always shied away from fish too. My kids still tease me about my unwavering loyalty to Clover Leaf tuna – solid, never flaked – the only fish I regularly eat. Since I didn't serve fish to my boys growing up, it was a great surprise to me when my older son expressed his love for sushi a few years ago. He suggested this feat to introduce me to what he was sure would be a whole new world of culinary pleasure for me.

On his recommendation, we went to Raw Fish in St. Catharines for all-you-can-eat lunch. The restaurant had pretty little hanging Japanese lanterns, and wooden booths with Christmas stockings hanging from the rafters to give it an extra festive feel. Our server asked us if we had been there before to determine how much she needed to explain. She showed me that the order form on the table was perforated so that we could order our courses in stages. While I was clueless, my son was well versed in the ordering protocol and I took my lead from him. I began with Miso soup while we perused the menu and decided what else we would try.

Together we chose a variety of dishes including cucumber rolls, calamari, beef teriyaki, spicy chicken skewers, salmon rolls, mango and shrimp hand rolls, and eel. I diligently tried everything, starting with the least challenging chicken, beef, and cucumber. Next up was octopus. I have eaten calamari before, but nothing like this dish – for the first time it was real to me that this was an octopus: the tentacles were 6 inches long, and I could see the suckers through the thin batter. Down the hatch it went, followed by a generous swig from my water glass. It was rubbery, but not so bad. Then I tried the salmon sushi roll. The roll was pretty, with the pink salmon wrapped around the top. Unfortunately for me, pretty didn't translate into appealing according to my taste buds: as I swallowed, I experienced a gag response. My poor son looked very concerned and asked if I was okay. He then gave me the option of not trying anything else out of both genuine concern for me, and a realization that his ability to frequent the premises in future depended upon not having his lunch mate throw up at the table.

I did step back for a bit and filled up mostly on the chicken and beef dishes. But, my big finish was to try the eel that we had ordered. I think I might have swallowed this without chewing, but my adventuresome heart was in the right place. We ended our meal with green tea ice cream, which I kind of liked, or maybe disliked less than most of the other dishes.

In the end, I enjoyed lunch with my son, but, I confess, don't think you will see us out for another sushi meal anytime soon. I guess I am my mother's daughter, just not a "fish person" unless you count a little Miracle Whip and Clover Leaf solid white tuna.

December 6, 2015

#FABFEAT: TO PIERCE, OR NOT TO PIERCE

I am a 50-year-old woman. In my younger years, I was very shy and reserved, but as I grew older, I slowly gained my own voice, my own style. I enjoy dressing with colour and flare, appreciate the ability to express my individuality. On my 46th birthday, I got a tattoo to celebrate my life: a small rainforest frog, my spirit animal, representing transition and transformation, now graces my left ankle.

Given my comfort being somewhat of a free spirit, why, then, was I so hesitant about getting my nose pierced? I have considered it for several years. Every time I would see a cute little sparkling stud on a woman standing in line at the grocery store or sitting at the table across from me at my local coffee shop, I would think about getting one myself. But, I was always taken down by the voice in my head that suggested middle-aged Moms, especially those who worked in (or wished to gain employment in) professional positions, did not indulge in nose bling.

After a recent encounter with a woman close to my own age who seemed unfazed by any potential judgments about her nose piercing, I reflected again about my own discomfort. While my tattoo is easily covered, this change would be "out there" for all to see. What was my concern? That my age deemed me ineligible for facial piercing? That people might make negative assumptions about me based upon a tiny nose stud? I realized that I was making my choice because of how it might look to others rather than how it would feel for me. If the only consideration was my own desire, the answer would be a decisive yes.

Nonetheless, I sought input from a few of my friends and other acquaintances, all women of a certain age. When I expressed my interest in getting my nose pierced, there were no upraised eyebrows or cautionary directives. When I asked about my age, one woman shrugged her shoulders and told me she didn't see that as an issue. When I questioned the reaction of potential employers or consulting clients with another woman who runs her own business, she noted that they were all strangers to me, and they wouldn't know me any differently than the way I presented myself. Besides, she said, if your talent is being assessed based on a little nose stud, that might give you some idea about whether you want to work with them anyway. Good observation. Something I would likely say to someone who asked me a similar question.

So, armed with this new perspective, I picked up my older son, who generously serves as my companion for many of my Fabulous Feats, and drove to Artistic Impressions in St. Catharines. There I met a lovely man named Jeremy who said he could take me in right away. After filling out a couple of forms, I followed him into the back room where he explained the process: a swipe of sterile gauze, location selected, marked, and approved by me, a quick pinch from the needle, and, voila, done. And that is exactly how it went. He gave me instructions for aftercare which included sea salt water soaks to aid in healing. He also cautioned me to be watchful for such things as hugging a friend wearing an infinity scarf, as the stud can catch on the fabric. It seemed like an oddly specific warning.

I returned to the front and brought out my credit card to pay. Jeremy pointed to the framed poster above the register: cash only. I was clearly not the first person caught out by this requirement; he told me there was an ATM at the convenience store down the street. I left my purse and my son as collateral and ran down to get the cash. Upon my return, I joked that if it hadn't been for leaving my purse, I could have abandoned my son in a "pierce and run." Apparently, my son had predicted that I would make this comment upon my return. I'm nothing if not predictable.

Day 2 and I am already used to the feeling. The stud is so small that it is hardly noticeable. But, to me, it represents a little sparkle and shine – my inside spirit represented by my outside appearance. My only concern, keeping a keen eye out for those now dangerous infinity scarves.

February 9, 2016

#FABFEAT: COME FLY WITH ME!

I am afraid of heights. I have been for as long as I can remember. It's called acrophobia and is defined by Wikipedia as "an extreme or irrational fear or phobia of heights" and is likely something I was born with along with some of my other non-specific anxieties. So, when a friend at work wanted to go on the new Niagara Falls zip line in celebration of a significant birthday, my initial response was a quickening of my pulse at the mere thought of it. However, as Neale Donald Walsch suggests, "life begins at the edge of your comfort zone," and instead of backing away, I told her I was in!

It was the weekend after my friend Shirley's birthday that we decided we would take advantage of having Monday as a holiday by booking our adventure. She registered us and we both filled out our waiver forms (I confess to being a little anxious as I agreed that the activity "involves many inherent risks, dangers and hazards" followed by an exhaustive list of possibilities including "wildlife, falls, and collision with trees or structures." I decided it was best to not read the fine print too closely). Early that afternoon we were on our way to Niagara Falls.

The MistRider Zipline to the Falls is new this summer. It advertises "an amazing rush to soar high and fast towards the breathtaking natural Niagara Falls phenomenon." There are four 2,200 feet zip lines that run parallel to each other through the river gorge that promised a perfect view of the Canadian and American falls.

We made our way to the Zipline only to find that we had to check in at another building on the other side of Clifton Hill. It was a bit confusing, but we managed to find it after asking a second time. We checked in and asked about pictures that Shirley had been assured on the phone would be available today; we were more than a little devastated to find out the photographers were gone for the day. We asked to talk to a Manager since we didn't know if we wanted to go if we couldn't have "proof" of our journey. A young man named Matt met us and explained that the photos were just being pilot tested and there was no guarantee of when they might be available. When he saw our disappointment, he got out his own phone and showed us pictures that he and his Mom had taken themselves and assured us that we could easily get our own pictures with our phones. With this information, we decided we would continue with our plans and joined the others who were part of the 5 p.m. group.

As we waited in line, we struck up a conversation with the couple behind us. They were from New York and had decided to drive back tomorrow, leaving them time to try out the zip line this afternoon rather than battle the border traffic. As we received our helmets and took the elevator up to the landing, we chatted amiably with them about our unique celebration of Shirley's birthday. They laughed along with us when we told them that we worked in mental health and said they would enjoy going down the Zipline as a foursome to share our experience!

I watched the attendants leaning casually against the glass partition between the platform and the sky and felt my heart beat faster. For the first time since arriving, I quietly said, "I'm afraid of heights." Just a statement, not a game changer. I became a little more anxious as we donned our gear – a durable (I hoped) canvas seat and harness that you stepped into, clipped here and there around your body and attached to the pulley attached to the zip line. I half-jokingly asked the attendant to reassure me that they hadn't lost anyone yet. She looked to be less than half my age; she smiled and put her hand on my shoulder telling me, "You got this." I wasn't entirely sure this statement was true, but I was strapped in and ready to go; at this point there was only one way down.

The glass panel opened, and we were on our way. As previously discussed with our New York friends, we all screamed as we left the platform (I was glad I was able to scream since I had feared I would be catatonically silent). Then, everything became quiet. We were flying. Shirley, who had shot out in front of us for some unknown reason, later described her experience as feeling a lightness and serenity while enveloped in the tremendous roar of the wind. The journey takes less than a minute and reaches up to 60 kilometres an hour, but it felt to me like I was almost suspended in mid-air; the beautiful views of the gorge, the trees, the falls passed by as if in slow motion. I had no fear; it was peaceful.

At the bottom our foursome reconnected and we all spoke about how amazing our experiences had been. Shirley and I remained at the bottom for some time enjoying a view of the Falls from a vantage point that one of the attendants said had not been open to the public for more than 30 years. Finally, we conceded to get on the shuttle that took us back up the gorge. We looked at the pictures Shirley had taken and realized they were at least as good, if not better, than any we would have purchased, and we saved money in the end.

We continued to be in awe of our experience for the rest of the evening. Both Shirley and I are "mature" and experiencing transitions in our worlds, which resulted in not just the fun of zip lining, but also a more philosophical reflection on the life lessons that we could glean from our time in the air:

- When you are in flight, you can see in front of you and look around you, but you can't look back.
- You can experience your own serenity even when the world is roaring around you.

- New experiences can be scary at first, but once you take the step, the journey can be so worth it.
- Sometimes what you anticipate being essential before you begin turns out not to be important at all in the end.
- Experiences shared are double the fun!

My greatest of thanks to Shirley who helped me to once again live my life just a bit past my comfort zone.

September 12, 2016

PILLAR OF POSITIVITY #7:

Committing To Your Goals

When I type "committing to your goals" into Google, I get 176,000 results. There are thousands of books, blogs, posts, tips, courses, videos, not to mention personalized pillow cases, mugs, keychains, posters, bags, and buttons that promise the answer to achieving your life's objectives. While I have a healthy skepticism about the impact of an embroidered head rest, the benefits to determining and moving towards your personal intentions and desires are supported by research: increased self-esteem, confidence, better coping skills (especially during times of crisis), more social connections, and greater meaning and purpose in life.

The nature of the goals is also important, with those that are intrinsically motivated (that is, not based on external rewards) and specifically authentic to you providing the most positive results. Another key element to the power of goal setting is the idea of moving towards something you want rather than away from something undesirable; for example, it is better to pursue a new job from a place of contentment rather than to escape a bad situation.

My 50 Fabulous Feats experiment provided me with the opportunity to learn about and experience the positive advantages of setting and achieving goals that were personal, genuinely mine, and very much connected to my life's passion and purpose. As I look back, the goals I achieved over that year were significant: I completed my M.Ed., started a whole new "encore" career as a Mental Health Recovery Support Worker as well as my own consulting service, and was selected as a SPARKie, receiving training with the Mental Health Commission of Canada to bring my wellness project to a wider audience.

It is important to recognize that these accomplishments were only achieved by making a series of tiny goals and trusting myself to take those baby steps that got me just a little closer to the finish line. I had to tackle my fear of travelling alone to get to the SPARK training in Ottawa. I needed to successfully fight my impulse to flee and remain firmly planted in my seat in that first Master's class where the only other "mature" student was 27 years old. Every time I had doubts, fears, in some cases, flat out terror that I would never succeed, I went back to my overarching goal of pursuing my passion for mental health and wellbeing to make a positive impact on the people around me.

I'm not special in my abilities; the truth is that anyone can set and achieve goals. They don't have to be earth-shatteringly large and they definitely shouldn't be defined by what you think others would want you to achieve. Too many of the people I currently serve believe that they don't count in society because they aren't able to work at paid employment. The only thing that really matters is pursuing goals that are meaningful and rewarding for <u>you</u>. I pushed myself beyond my comfort zone because I believed in the value of my goals. Now I am also able to support others as they determine what is important in their lives; I am truly privileged!

There are many resources for setting goals that provide steps, templates, and support, but they all have a few things in common:

- **Why**: Think about your personal aspirations, intentions, and wishes (not what you think others might value or want you to do).
- **What**: Consider your priorities and pick <u>one</u> goal to target.
- **How**: Determine the actions you need to take to achieve this goal.
- **When**: Set some specific time frames for each step.
- **Who**: Reach out to people who can help you to stay on track, support you, provide feedback along the way, and celebrate your successes with you.

I'd love to hear about your goals and support you along the way through your Fabulous Feats.

"life begins at the edge of your comfort zone." – Neale Donald Walsch

May 24, 2017

#FABFEAT: FACILITATING A WORLD CAFÉ

Did you read the title of this feat and think "what?" If so, you are not alone, which could have been slightly problematic since I was, in fact, one of the people who was to be doing the facilitating.

Here's the story: As I am currently exploring career opportunities, I have been reaching out to friends and colleagues to gather guidance and knowledge based upon their experiences. I am privileged to have wonderful people in my life who have been generous with their time and wisdom when I ask to meet and "pick their brains" of useful and sage advice. During one recent chat, a friend suggested he had a need for some facilitators for a workshop he was running and asked if I was interested. Normally I am somewhat risk averse, and would have hesitated at the offer, but, in keeping with my new 50 Feats motto, I immediately responded "I'm in!"

The following week I received an email outlining the task: facilitating a modified world cafe on the topic of physician-hospital partnerships. I admit that the blood drained from my face since I was neither familiar with the format nor the topic. However, instead of finding some excuse to beat a hasty retreat, I turned to the Internet to get a sense of just what I was getting myself into. It turns out that a world cafe is an organizational workshop designed to open creative sharing of knowledge on a topic of mutual interest often used with large groups. When I understood the concept, I realized that I had facilitated numerous similar discussions during my Human Resources career. With respect to hospital -physician partnerships, I turned to the research literature and, after reading several articles, I had a general sense of the topic and its challenges.

Armed with somewhat of a framework, on the day of the workshop I tackled the next challenge – finding the venue. Anyone who knows me is painfully aware of how directionally challenged I am. However, the creation of the GPS has been my salvation and, just to be sure I would end up where I was supposed to be, I updated my maps in advance of setting out for my destination, adding a cushion of 45 minutes in the event of the inevitable missed turns, construction, and potential parking challenges. Much to my surprise, I managed only one wrong turn, and was parked, oriented and settled well in advance of my necessary arrival time.

When I entered the meeting room, I knew only my friend, who was engaged in his presentation preparation, and his partner who was also facilitating at the session. Everyone else was involved in the setup of tables and chairs so I jumped in and helped. By the time participants began arriving, I felt somewhat comfortable, that is, until the facilitators gathered, and we introduced ourselves. Each person said their name and a bit about their background: 36

years in organizational development in a hospital setting; former hospital administrator and current consultant for the healthcare sector; nurse educator with 25 years of experience...I admit to feeling somewhat intimidated, but, when it was my turn, I told them of my 25 years in university administration and my almost completed Master's degree related to coaching and mentoring. I looked around and was relieved to see no horrified or dismissive expressions or questioning of my lack of hospital experience – first hurdle overcome.

We were assigned our tables and questions that would form the basis of discussions; I was thankful that I had done my research since my groups would be working on the possible format of a hospital-physician partnership agreement. I introduced myself to the participants as they arrived and was feeling relatively comfortable about my ability to get through the next two hours. That is, until the final individual took his seat at my table – he was the hospital CEO. Yikes! I took a deep breath and reminded myself that he was simply another participant, and I was an experienced facilitator. I also remembered the advice of one of my early career mentors: whatever happens, act is if it is what you planned because no one else knows any different.

The next couple of hours moved along quickly. I facilitated the discussions and recorded a summary of the dialogue for the first table, then recapped and continued the process for two subsequent 20-minute sessions as the table participants shifted to the left giving everyone a chance to answer all three of the questions being considered.

I was even able to connect with a couple of the other facilitators who suggested we stay in touch regarding our interests and consulting opportunities as we were interested in similar kinds of work and research.

As I walked to my car at the end of the evening, I felt quite buoyed by my accomplishment. Instead of second guessing what I might have done differently as I often did in the past, I took the time to just feel good about my performance. I reflected on the feats I have completed so far and realized that each time I stretch myself a little more doing things that interest me, I broaden my skills, experiences, and comfort with taking the next leap; this is what Dr. Barbara Fredrickson identified in her broaden and build theory of positive emotions. My positive psychology experiment is in full swing!

November 21, 2015

#FABFEAT: SCHOOL'S OUT!

When I began my Master of Education program full-time in September of 2014 I could hardly think past the next day, let alone to its successful completion. While I am a voracious reader, and had taken the odd course here and there, it had been over 25 years since I had completed my undergraduate degree. But, I had always wanted to do graduate work, so when I was downsized out of my job, I felt like the Universe might be giving me a little nudge to really take my life in a new direction.

I applied, was accepted, and found myself joining the rush of university students, shiny new backpack full of text books slung over my shoulder, as I walked to my first graduate class that Fall. When I entered the room, I was struck by how young my classmates looked. In fact, most were freshly out of their undergraduate education programs, returning to school while they tried to break into teaching during a time when jobs were scarce to say the least. In one class, we were to introduce ourselves and tell each other one interesting fact about ourselves- I blurted out that I was old enough to be everyone else's Mom. Smooth.

It is true that it took me until November to stop saying "whatever made me think this was a good idea," but when I did, I realized I was loving my experience. When I completed my undergraduate degree, I really wasn't sure what I wanted to do with my life. I enjoyed psychology, perhaps because it focused on human dynamics, which I found fascinating. I took a personnel psych course and then applied to a summer program as a student in personnel (SIP). I was fortunate enough to be hired to work at the University of Toronto in their Human Resources department and spent the next 4 months thrown into the world of HR. I interviewed candidates, conducted salary surveying, and became hooked on HR as a profession. I began my first real HR job a week before my convocation, and spent the next 26 years there.

While I loved working in HR, because I worked in a university, I sometimes thought about how much I had loved researching and writing as an undergrad. But my life was full, with work and family, and it wasn't until 2009 that I started taking courses towards a Bachelor of Education in Adult Education. When life again became too busy, I shelved my courses after completing only 2 of the required 5. When my job ended, after the initial grieving, I chose to look for the opportunity – school was the obvious answer for me.

As I now look back over the last 15 months, I am humbled by the experiences I was able to participate in as part of my programming: research into the elimination of self-stigma surrounding mental illness; a directed study at the hospital mental health unit related to the impact of positive psychology tools in enhancing mood (which spurred my 50 Feats); an internship with a local women's addiction recovery organization where I developed a holistic aftercare curriculum; and my final culminating project that explored the potential for a combined coaching and mentoring model to support the success of early career academics.

Throughout the experience, I was continually impressed by my young and talented classmates – they were keen, friendly, inclusive, smart, funny, and committed. I know each one will make their own unique and positive impact on the world in the years to come. I learned with them and from them and feel very privileged to have met them all.

My final poster presentation seemed almost surreal to me. Could I really have completed my M.Ed. requirements? We had a little celebration as part of our class time, and everyone looked both as tentative and relieved as I felt. As we filed out of the room at the end of the night, I confess to feeling just a little empty too.

Like all graduates, I am now back to the real world of looking for employment. But, my heart is still that of a student and I'm not yet ready to completely give up that rediscovered world: a few days ago, I signed up for the 3rd of my online Adult Education courses that I abandoned in 2010. Do what you love; love what you do.

December 29, 2015

#FABFEAT: MEET THE NEW BOSS

As this is the mid-point of my 50 Fabulous Feats, I thought a long time about what this week's activity would be. I have been interviewed for a couple of positions recently, and wondered if this blog might announce the beginning of my next career direction. It turns out that, while I wasn't the successful candidate for any of the positions for which I was being considered, this posting is still all about revealing my new path.

Over the last year and a half, I have been able to be self-directed through the course of completing my Master's studies. Throughout my graduate work, I completed course papers, internships, and directed studies. I organized my priorities, managed my time, and created materials based upon research and my own creativity. I rekindled my passion for learning and loved the ability to consider the bigger picture, then break down the project to its component parts. I felt privileged to be able to focus on mental health and addiction education and advocacy for many of my assignments. I loved the fact that my workplace alternated between the library and my very own dining room table.

Looking back over this time, I realized that at least one answer to my job search was to continue in this same direction. Instead of looking outwards, I can spend some time working on my own business, setting up my own consulting business, with particular focus on Human Resources solutions and mental health education, thereby merging the skills from my "old life" with the capacities I have developed in my "new life." I know that I am in the very early stages of fulfilling this dream. I will need to learn the ropes including everything from developing my business plan, to understanding the legal requirements, to determining marketing strategies. Every consultant I have talked to so far has been quick to tell me two things: they love being their own boss and it is incredibly hard work to be self-employed. I know that it will be a challenge, but when I think back over the last few years, I realize that I have a pretty good track record with overcoming obstacles and turning trials into triumphs.

I welcome all insights, suggestions, words of wisdom, and cautionary tales from those who have already walked this career pathway. In February of last year, I began SilverLiningFrog.com; I can't wait to see what it will look like a year from now: the sky is the limit!

February 1, 2016

#FABFEAT: PUT ME IN, COACH!

During my career in Human Resources, I have had the opportunity to try my hand at number of different functions. Over the years I discovered areas that I loved and those that drained my energy. Interestingly, Employee Relations fell into both those buckets. While I found investigations, discipline, and dismissal incredibly difficult, the flip side was being able to work one-on-one with individuals where I could support them to become their best selves. It is not surprising, therefore, that when I began my own consulting business, I was drawn to coaching and mentoring as a possible niche. But, even though I had lots of practical involvement from my previous work, I was concerned that I didn't have specific education in coaching; I didn't want to give less than the best experience for people who might want to hire me as a coach.

My go-to response to this dilemma was to do some research on coaching courses. Since there is no regulatory body outside of athletics coaching, there are many courses and individuals who have hung up their shingles, calling themselves everything from Life Coaches to Personal Coaches to Solution-Focused Coaches. After a little searching, I found a couple of organizations that provided coaching certification training. The Certified Coaching Federation (CCF) appeared to be one that had been around for a while and respected. When I looked up the courses available, I was excited to find an intensive certification course was scheduled in Niagara Falls in April. I decided to make the investment and signed up.

A few days before the two-day session, the instructor contacted me to let me know the location (which turned out to be just down the street from me) and what to expect. There were 8 people enrolled and we would be working from 9 to 6 on Saturday and Sunday, including working lunches. As we chatted, I discovered that Sam, and her partner Chris, we're opening a holistic wellness centre in Niagara Falls called Grounded Roots Wellness which will include coaching, DDP yoga, float pod therapy, salt rooms, infrared sauna, fitness and nutrition. As well, Sam told me she was a psychic medium and spiritual advisor. We had a great conversation and I was excited about the training.

On the first day of the course I was the first to arrive. The wellness centre was not yet open so we were set up in a large open space that also housed giant plastic-covered objects that I later found out were the float pods which were awaiting set-up. Sam greeted me and was as bubbly and welcoming as she had been on the phone. Shortly, others began to arrive, and we settled in to begin the day.

We started by introducing ourselves and telling others something interesting about ourselves. I, of course, mentioned my blog site. It was a very diverse group with backgrounds that included financial, fitness, corporate sales, and human resources. We spent the morning learning a little about the coaching process, and soon were partnered up and role-playing client and coach. Using a framework of questions provided, we discussed our goals and gained more bang for our buck by not only practicing the coaching role, but receiving personal coaching ourselves in the process. Our homework was to craft the information we gleaned into a script that we would share with our coaching partners the next day and, thereby, tap into their subconscious through painting a picture of the successful accomplishment of their goals.

Day 2 began with an individual review of our scripts by Sam which allowed me time to chat with the woman who was sitting beside me. The Universe does work in mysterious ways and it turned out that she and I had many things in common, including a passion for supporting mentally healthy individuals. It was wonderful to talk to her about her experiences and the opportunities she was exploring, and I have no doubt that she will bring magic and healing to the world.

It was then time to share our scripts with our coaching partners. I was very taken by how much I was motivated by the description of my goal success; my mind was able visualize all the steps as

I listened to the description. When I read the script I had developed for my partner, she was tearful and I realized how powerful this process could be. By the end of the second day we had moved from complete strangers to colleagues and friends. We had a small "graduation" ceremony and everyone contributed heartfelt cheers in support of our success as newly certified coach practitioners.

As I reflected on the experience that evening, I felt energized and confident about my ability to support others in developing an understanding of and a path for accomplishing their goals. Another exciting feat fulfilled!

April 13, 2016

#FABFEAT: ACTT-ING FOR THE REGION

Since returning to school and focusing much of my M.Ed. studies on mental health education, I have had the goal of transitioning to a new career that includes working in the field of mental health. Through my volunteer work with Canadian Mental Health Association – Niagara, I have had the opportunity to meet many individuals who are living with mental illness. While we each have our own unique experiences, there is often a connection on a visceral level as our struggles and successes resonate with someone else who has "been there." I recognize that I am not a clinician with respect to mental illness, but I have felt that a peer-to-peer relationship can provide a special kind of support.

According to the Mental Health Commission of Canada, peer support is proven to be both an effective and cost efficient method of assisting individuals living with mental illness (http://www.mentalhealthcommission.ca/English/issues/peer-support): "Empowerment and the development of personal resourcefulness — the foundation of peer support — not only improves people's lives but also saves money by reducing the use of more formal mental health, medical, and social services."

So, when I saw that The Niagara Region's Public Health department was advertising for a Recovery Support Worker in the Mental Health Unit, I was excited about the possibility. The Assertive Community Treatment Team (ACTT) is designed to assist individuals with the most serious and persistent mental illness, including schizophrenia and bipolar disorder. Individuals supported by this service often have co-existing problems such as homelessness, substance abuse or involvement with the judicial system.

I excitedly applied for the role in November of last year, and was sure that the position had been filled when I received an email invitation to interview in mid-March. I felt very positive about the interview and the Managers who were on the hiring committee and was beyond thrilled to be offered the job a few weeks later. I accepted with great enthusiasm and more than a little nervousness; I would be both new to this job and to the field of direct service in the mental health field.

My start date quickly arrived – it felt like the first day of school. The night before I woke up every hour, checking the clock fearing I might oversleep. I consciously completed my work attire with earrings and a necklace that had been given to me by people I love, thereby creating my own Linus blanket and providing me with a little comfort to assuage my nervousness. My car seemed to know exactly which way to drive after spending so many years travelling to Brock University for work and, more recently, for school; I just had to remember to turn left just a bit sooner to make my way to the Region.

My anxiety was quickly lessened as I was greeted by welcoming colleagues. My day began with the regular team meeting, followed by a whirlwind tour of the Welland and Niagara Falls sites, and the opportunity to accompany one member of my team on her client visits in the afternoon. I was struck by how she connected with each of the individuals in a caring and respectful manner. While I felt overwhelmed by my own inexperience working directly with clients in a mental health setting, I was confident I was in the right workplace.

The following two days I travelled to Welland to job shadow with the other Recovery Support Worker who was the original peer support person on the team and had chosen to work in Welland where she lived when the second ACT team was created there. She had been in her role for the last 10 years, and had previously worked with CMHA. I was awed by her calm, caring approach to everyone she met, and her connection with the clients she visited. I was thankful to have the opportunity to observe her while she worked, and especially for the time she took to talk with me about the role, her approach and the importance of peer support. I was grateful for her kind words of encouragement when I expressed my fears about being able to provide worthy support and connection to the people I would be serving and to adequately represent the perspective of individuals living with mental illness on the team.

As I write this blog, I have completed my first week at my new job. My brain is full each evening, but so is my heart. I know I have a lot of learning still to do, and that I am privileged to have been given an opportunity to work in this capacity; I will endeavor to earn the trust I have been given by fulfilling the role to the very best of my ability, providing support, empowerment, and hope to those who are in need.

April 24, 2016

#FABFEAT: 50 FEATS - THE WORKSHOP

In addition to presenting 50 Feats @ 50 through my blog, I have been exploring ways of spreading the message of using novel, intentional, personally interesting experiences to positively impact mood. My adventures have been so fulfilling that I feel strongly about sharing with others, especially individuals who, like me, have sometimes struggled with low affect due to mental illness (for me, anxiety and depression).

I was given my first opportunity to sing the joys of 50 Feats recently when I was describing my blog to one of the organizers of the Niagara Talking About Mental Illness (TAMI) program after a TAMI presentation to a high school class in St. Catharines. She suggested that I deliver 50 Feats as a professional development workshop at the next TAMI Speakers' Meeting. I immediately agreed – particularly since May seemed so far away! And then, it was here, so I spent a Saturday working through the format and creating my PowerPoint slides.

I was able to categorize my feats using Sonja Lyubormirsky's pillars from The Myth of Happiness: expressing gratitude; cultivating optimism; practicing acts of kindness; nurturing social relationships; developing coping strategies; savouring life's joys; committing to your goals;

and taking care of your mind, body, and spirit. I noted the benefits of each grouping that had been identified through the research and then included the feats completed to date that primarily fit into each category (many were overlapping in possible placement). As the presentation developed, I relived the experiences and reflected on how my feelings of positivity, increased energy, and wellbeing paralleled the research findings; my positive psychology experiment was working!

The true test of the workshop came on a Monday night when I stood in front of my fellow TAMI presenters as well as several Public Health Promoters from the Region. Having never delivered this workshop, I was somewhat nervous about how it would unfold. I had 45 minutes and was unsure of my exact timing, particularly because I tend to wander and expand on themes when I become excited about the topic. I began by talking about positive psychology, the concept behind SilverLiningFrog.com, and the origins of 50 Fabulous Feats before moving into the positive psychology pillars and the feats the that fit within them. I was excited as I described the benefits and my amazing experiences. Before I knew it, 40 minutes had passed, and I had to turn the interactive excrcise that had participants creating their own list of fabulous feats into a take-home project.

As I took what may have been my first breath in 45 minutes, I concluded the workshop by inviting questions. One of the young women who speaks in the TAMI program commented that she and her mother had attended feat #14 Speaking Out About Mental Health at Brock where I spoke from the perspective of a parent providing support to my young adult son as he dealt with the onset of bipolar disorder. She had tears in her eyes as she told me how affected her mother was by listening to another mother talk about the struggles and challenges. I also experienced a few tears during our exchange; the positive psychology connection was felt once again by both giver and receiver.

The evening concluded with our regular Speakers' Meeting, but the glow from my presentation lasted well beyond the actual delivery – as I write this, I can feel the warmth all over again.

The next day, I received feedback from two of the Health Promoters in emails celebrating my 'fabulous and inspiring' feats and the value of being present in one's own life. I, in turn, am inspired by them and my fellow TAMI presenters who make a positive difference in the lives of high school students with every presentation they provide and the personal stories of recovery they share.

As I write this, I have just completed my third week as a Recovery Support Worker with Niagara Region Mental Health. In addition, it is Mother's Day and

I am off to have dinner with my two beautiful boys. I continue to experience gratitude for my many blessings, and savour the wonders of my life. Wishing all my family, friends, and community a very Happy Mother's Day.

May 9, 2016

#FABFEAT: CROSSING THE STAGE

This week's feat was a big one for me. Having completed the academic requirements for my Master of Education degree in December of last year, the day had finally arrived for me to celebrate this milestone by donning a gown and hood, and crossing the stage to receive my diploma.

As exciting was the fact that my younger son would be cheering me on from the audience, and my older son there in spirit (crowds are not his thing), but, thankfully, also at home again after a short hospital stay.

We arrived at Brock just after 1 p.m. and I made my way to the area marked "Graduates" with a big smile; I collected my gown and with a sigh of relief found my name on a convocation card on the gym wall that confirmed I really was going to cross that stage.

I wasn't sure if I would know anyone else, having completed my last course in the Fall of 2015, but was happily surprised to see several familiar faces. We had ample time to catch up as we waited for the 2:30 procession. I celebrated with my classmates as they described their achievements in work and life since finishing their degrees. Each time someone asked me about my plans, I flushed with the excitement of describing my new position at Niagara Region

Mental Health and how privileged I feel to have been given the role of Recovery Support Worker there.

Soon, we were lined up in alphabetical order and began the procession. As I walked down the hallway, my friend Karen popped out with her phone and took my picture while wishing me a heartfelt congratulation. I felt myself getting just a little misty-eyed. As we walked to our seats, I spotted my son in the crowd (wearing a bright green shirt turned out to have been a good idea) and gave a wave; more waterworks threatened.

We awaited the procession of the platform party and, since the M.Ed.'s were the first degrees to be conferred, we were soon on our feet and making our way to the side of the stage. I passed my son along the way and was rewarded with a high five that again brought a few joyful tears. We snaked up the ramp to the podium and, as I walked onto the stage, I was overwhelmed by the friendly faces of former Brock colleagues. One gave me the hooding instructions (don't shake hands with the Bedels – it slows things down too much); another read my name aloud; others shook my hand and congratulated me as I made my way across the stage. I may have held up those behind me for just a bit, but having worked for many years with some of these individuals, I was delighted as each person jumped up with outstretched hands.

The best was saved to the last as my beautiful friend, The Registrar, enveloped me in a hug as I received my diploma – cue the water works! I floated back to my seat and, upon opening the diploma folder to just make sure it really was true, I found not only the M.Ed. document, but a card from my friend tucked in the corner; as others around me took a second look in their folders, I confess to feeling pretty special.

The rest of the ceremony was uneventful for me. As we made our way outside, I looked for my former colleague and always dear friend, Margo, whose convocation I had proudly attended last year. I had to leave before we found each other because I had promised Christian that his brother and I would pick him up for a celebratory dinner and he was awaiting our arrival (virtual hugs to Margo for always being in my corner).

The dinner topped off an exceptional day. As I watched my boys kibitz over their meals, I quietly reflected on the many, many blessings in my life. Sending out love and immense gratitude to all my supporters, especially over the last two years – I couldn't have done any of it without you!

June 13, 2016

#FABFEAT: BECOMING A SPARKIE: PART 2 -THE TRAINING

Having arrived in Ottawa without any difficulty, I was ready to take on the main phase of my SPARKie experience. The first evening was a meet-and-greet, dinner, and an introduction by two of the workshop presenters. I was able to get to know a few my fellow SPARKies as well as some of the mentors and MHCC staff members at the reception where we played getting-to-know-you Bingo; I was pleased to be able to sign other's cards for both "a parent" and "has a tattoo." I admit to being a little intimidated by the stories of the other participants – Research Coordinator at CAMH; Executive Director, CMHA Alberta; Regional Manager, Disability Services; Master's and PhD students. Me, oh, I run my own personal blog site! Nonetheless, everyone was inclusive and wonderful and some of my anxiety dissipated.

After a lovely dinner, we were introduced to our keynote speakers: Dr. Elliot Goldner is a psychiatrist and Dr Dan Bilsker is a psychologist; both are connected with the Centre for Applied Research in Mental Health and Addictions (CARMHA) at Simon Fraser University (Dan is also a professor at University of British Columbia) and co-authored Innovation to Implementation (I2I), the knowledge translation guide that we will be using during the workshop. When they took to the stage, it was abundantly clear that I was with kindred spirits. Yes, they were talented, intelligent, and expert in knowledge translation, but Dan and Elliot were also funny and engaging, playing off each other in a way that showed how much they enjoyed working together. As the evening concluded with a wonderful Aboriginal dance performance, I walked back to my room eagerly anticipating the start of SPARK training 2016.

Upon entering the training room in the morning, I saw that each participant was directed to a table based upon their assigned mentor. I had not met my mentor the previous evening, but had read his description in the SPARK bios. Dr. David Wiljer is the Senior Director of Transformational Education and Academic Advancement at the Centre for Addictions and Mental Health as well as a professor at University of Toronto. Whew! That feeling of unworthiness returned, bringing with it some nervousness as I anticipated our meeting. The gentle man who joined our table and introduced himself as David turned out to be approachable, funny, and a delight to work with over the next two days (in addition to being as knowledgeable and impressive as his bio suggested!).

Day 1 began with an overview of the I2I. Earlier in June, SPARKies had been given access to the modules online and so I had a bit of an idea about the process of Innovation to Implementation, but it was through working with fellow participants, and putting pen to paper as it related to my own SilverLiningFrog project that solidified my commitment to and passion for contributing to "closing the gap between what we know and what we do." I believe I provide living proof of the value of adopting positive psychology techniques to increase positive emotions, and I want to motivate others to not just travel vicariously through my Fabulous Feats, but to engage in their own activities in support of their own wellbeing, especially for those who may, like me, struggle with mental health challenges. I realized how privileged I was to have the opportunity to learn how to effectively move forward with my project based upon the I2I model and with access to the expertise of mentors, SPARK staff, and the feedback from my fellow participants.

By the end of the first day, I had a purpose statement: To promote understanding and motivate the adoption of positive psychology evidence-based practices to increase individuals' positive emotions, foster mental wellbeing, hope and possibilities, particularly for those living with mental illness.

Day 2 provided the opportunity to create a "bird's-eye view of our KT plans that we would present and receive feedback on in our mentor groups. I was able to envision my project from a multi-phased perspective: SilverLiningFrog.com and my 50+ Fabulous Feats (my mentor David suggested that I needed to add the "+" to ensure that the feats continued!) was at the centre of disseminating the information about my positive psychology practices, and could be expanded to include such things as an interactive website where others could post about their own experiences, a workshop that provides information about the various kinds of positive psychology practices and encourages participants to determine their own "feats" and report back on their progress, and developing "Feats Coaching" with individuals, particularly those who may be struggling with mental illness. With encouragement from my fellow SPARKies, I also thought about other forms of dissemination such as webinars, whiteboard presentations, a book or zine. After presenting my outline, I realized that I was no longer feeling like an imposter with a blog site, but a SPARKie with a mission!

The feeling of belonging came from a combination of creating a vision of my project and being infused with the support I received from everyone I met during the training. It would take another complete blog to describe the connections, conversations, and camaraderie I experienced in those two days, not to mention the amazing projects that were being developed by my SPARKie friends. Fortunately, the journey doesn't end with the completion of the workshop. Our mentor group will continue to check in with each other's progress, and I will be preparing my KT plan for my mentor's review as I embark on my project implementation that will take shape over the next year.

As I write this blog, the original excitement I felt during the workshop is building simply through reliving the memories. Since returning home, I have discussed the possibility of bringing the 50+ Feats experience to colleagues at my workplace and met with enthusiasm from the Human Resources representative. As I build my KT plan, I will determine a phased approach to the various opportunities and narrow in on the next steps. Stay tuned, while this blog represents Feat #41, 50+ Feats is just getting started!

July 24, 2016

PILLAR OF POSITIVITY #8:
Taking Care Of Your Body – Exercise

It is fitting that the positivity pillar of **taking care of your body** arrives just as summer is upon us. Everywhere you look, advertisements for a multitude of diets, pills, potions and lotions promise the ideal, sculpted beach body. While it is true that I am aware of a certain snugness in my summer clothing, this wellness focus is so much more than shedding a few pounds. Mind and body are inextricably connected for all of us. For someone who lives with depression and anxiety, the importance of looking after my physical health is especially important; nutrition, sleep hygiene, and exercise are critical to my overall wellbeing.

As good as I realize it is for me, I know that I am not alone in feeling less than enthusiastic when exercise comes up. I think that is because I associate exercise with the pained faces I see on various runners, weight lifters, spinners, and assorted gym junkies. While I recognize that these individuals may well be enjoying their workouts, I have not found my fulfillment in such activities.

I really had to define exercise for myself in a way that made it a positive experience rather than a "must do" in order for it to gain any traction in my life. For many years it was walking at lunch with friends; the interesting conversation that accompanied our time together often made me forget about the actual walking part. More recently, I have discovered a new kind of routine using mindfulness and walking in nature as my way of staying active. At times, I walk with my IPod and my favourite tunes, singing along when the feeling moves me (although I cannot, as my mother would say, carry a tune in a bucket, I happily belt out the lyrics like a rock star). On other occasions, I simply take in all the sights, sounds, and even smells that I encounter along the way. Yes, I actually do stop and smell the roses at times, as well as the lilacs, lily-of-the-valley, and a daisy or two. I listen to the songs of birds and of playing children, the swish of the wind in the trees, and feel the sun on my arms or the rain on my hair. Once again, I lose myself in the moments.

The benefits of exercise are well researched: better physical and mental health both during and after physical activity including reduced stress and anxiety; social connection; increased lifespan. Some research even supports that physical exercise can have as much, and sometimes more, of an effect in improving depression as anti-depressant medication. Exercise is also linked to improved memory, better quality of sleep, not to mention weight loss, reduction in chronic pain, and, wait for it, improved sex drive, performance, and pleasure.

The great thing about exercise is that there are so many alternatives to choose from based upon individual interests. Maybe you like team sports – hockey, softball, soccer. Perhaps swimming is your love. You may wish to attend Zumba classes, or to participate in yoga or Tai Chi. The beauty of exercise is there is no wrong answer (okay, watching sports on TV may be the exception). Just do it!

> *"Exercise not only changes your body,*
> *it changes your mind, your attitude and*
> *your mood." – Author Unknown*

July 9, 2017

#FABFEAT: CALL ME ISHMAEL

I have always been a "bookworm." As a shy child, reading was my refuge. In Grade 1, I read more books than anyone else in my class. My reward was having the opportunity to read aloud to the principal. My love of books was so strong that it outweighed my normally crippling anxiety and I remember proudly reading to Principal Chalmers.

Reading for me has always been my favourite form of play. Sure, I built forts, and rode my bike like my friends, but nothing could engage me like diving into a book. According to play researcher Stuart Brown, there are several universal principles of play: it is seemingly without purpose, voluntary in nature, inherently attractive, suspends time, diminishes consciousness of self, inspires improvisation, and instills a desire to continue the activity. Reading for me was the purest form of play.

It makes sense, therefore, that reading would form part of my 50 Feats selections. While I enjoy all genres, I missed out on some of the "classic" books. This gap led me to this feat – Herman Melville's Moby Dick. I decided to combine reading with walking and so downloaded the Moby Dick audio file to my phone and began my journey.

Perhaps I should have taken a better look at the length of the recording before beginning my feat.

Melville, it turns out, is a very (very) descriptive writer. His tale of a white whale ran just short of 26 hours of audio covering 135 chapters (and an epilogue). Initially, I was intrigued by the relationship between the narrator, Ishmeal, and the "tattooed cannibal," Queequag. I enjoyed the clever wordplay as he described the development of their unlikely friendship ("Throwing aside the counterpane, there lay the tomahawk sleeping by the savage's side, as if it were a hatchet-faced baby.").

Unfortunately, Melville's detailed descriptions were not limited to the interchange between characters. There were chapters devoted to identifying various types of whales, every nook and cranny of a whaling vessel, and, yes, more descriptions of whales. Much as I tried to stay in the moment, I confess to sometimes getting lost in my thoughts rather than focusing on the audio.

Overall, Moby Dick was not what my mother might have referred to as "my cup of tea." Yet, I was able to take away a few positives from the experience:

- From the book: I discovered that "scuttlebutt" is the barrel on a ship that holds fresh water for the day. As the sailors passed buckets to fill the scuttlebutt, they gossiped back and forth with each other.
- From the method: I learned that I enjoyed listening to audiobooks. While, like e-books, audiobooks will never completely replace

my love of turning the pages of a good, solid novel, I found a new way to enjoy "reading."
- From the experience: I walked for almost 26 hours by combining the audio book with my daily walks, increasing my stamina in preparation for my next feat of walking around the Isle of Wight.

Would I consider this a successful feat? While I doubt that Melville will be my next poolside read, I enjoyed the process; reading is never a waste. And, if sometime in the future a life depends upon knowing the difference between a blue and a right whale, I am so your leviathan savant.

August 13, 2015

#FABFEAT: 'ROUND THE ISLE OF WIGHT

Those of you who have been reading my 50 Feats blogs so far may be wondering: "When do the death defying, heart-stopping adventures begin?" My friends, I give you Fabulous Feat #5, a week-long walking tour of the Isle of Wight.

While my first few activities were mostly cerebral and reflective, this feat turned out to be all about physical endurance. I enjoy walking, but my exercise level has recently dropped to a dog's paced stroll rather than a workout. Still, I consider myself to be in shape, albeit closer to pear-shaped than any other.

Since I have no sense of direction, this adventure was not one that I could achieve on my own; it was definitely a "Feat with a Friend" activity. My walking companion, the Navigator, is a lifelong distance runner and this walking vacation was his idea. He suggested I review the Isle of Wight walking tours website for details of the distances, and route profile in advance of committing to the trip. I looked at the cute little map of the Isle and thought "How hard could it be?" Perhaps I should have done the bit of math that divided the 104 km covered by the Coastal Path we would be following into our 6 days of walking to realize the gravity of my commitment.

I was not completely oblivious to the physical requirements of the journey; I increased my daily walks to about an hour, sometimes two, each day in the weeks leading up to our departure. And so, I felt somewhat confident stepping off the ferry to begin the 6-day hiking holiday around the Isle of Wight via the Coastal Path.

The first day in Ryde was a "non-walking day". We settled in with an ad hoc 16 km "stroll" in the afternoon along the shore pathway which was tiring for me, but reasonably manageable. In the morning we were greeted with a full English breakfast and an overview of the trek ahead. Each day we would have our luggage shuttled to the next destination B&B, and we would walk the Coastal Path with just our rucksacks and a map guiding us up cliff hills, across pastures, over stiles, through villages, and down wooden stair pathways.

Over our time on the Isle (including the trail, a few sidetracks due to some missed turns along the way, and the walking around villages in the evenings), we covered more than 150 km with our longest days adding up to over 30 km! I found the walking incredibly challenging (while The Navigator not only completed the days effortlessly, but also got up in the mornings to go for a run prior to beginning our daily route – I would have been jealous were I not so tired). During the hours of walking, I considered a few thoughts about the journey that also translate nicely into life lessons:

- You're tougher than you think you are: when you think you can't go another step, I discovered that you can, sometimes hundreds more.

- Despite the above, sometimes it's okay to cry "uncle": on those occasions where I had to have a rest before carrying on, I simply plopped down on the grass and enjoyed the view for a few minutes.

- A healthy perspective is all about balance: if you spend all of your time looking down at your feet, you miss the beauty of the scenery, but if you are always looking at the view, you can easily stumble on a root. Alternating the two outlooks provides maximum pleasure with fewer falls. And sometimes, the beauty is right beside you if you simply take a moment to notice. Life's like that too.

- Take the time to celebrate your accomplishments: on particularly steep hills, I stopped at the top to relish my victory (okay, and gulp air like a fish out of water).

- The bridge you wish for isn't always there: sometimes you must go up the hill, only to come back down again. It is, however, okay to grumble under your breath.

- Your imagination can be your salvation: to take my mind off the aches and pains, I distracted myself with made-up stories about people we passed, sang songs in my head, and, more than a few times, pretended that

The Inexhaustible Navigator walking easily ahead of me was my Sherpa guide leading me up Everest.

- Sometimes you just have to fake it till you make it: by the end of the first day I knew I hadn't prepared enough for this walking tour, but I broke it up in my head into manageable chunks and then just kept on truckin' till my body was toned (okay, it turned out to be swelling from edema, but still) and my breathing easier.
- Have fun, and share it: I had a little Kermit in my backpack and took pictures of him at the various sites, posting his adventures for my friends to vicariously enjoy the trip.
- Savour the journey, because, in the end, we all finish in the same place we began: the walk started and ended in Ryde, but it was the sights, sounds, and encounters along the way that made the trip memorable.

Of course, my favourite part of the adventure was meeting people along the way – on the path, in the pubs, in the endless queues at the airports. The people on the Isle (natives are known as Corkheads) were lovely; they have a delightful way of making every statement into a subtle kind of question by adding an inflected "yah" on the end of a sentence. For example, one young woman sent us on our way with a breezy "You'll enjoy your walk, yah?" suggesting we would likely have an excellent time, while leaving the slightest possibility that we might plummet to our deaths off the narrow cliff pathway. See, I told you this was a death-defying feat!

Would I recommend this Fabulous Feat? A resounding YES. I am still a little sore and have a few bruises and blisters to remind me of the challenge, but it was an incredible experience that will provide a lifetime of memories. If you, too, are interested in becoming a "Wight Walker" (GOT pun intended), details can be found at http://www.visitisleofwight.co.uk/things-to-do/activities/walking (Sherpa not included).

August 24, 2015

#FABFEAT: WHAM, BAM, THANK YOU MAMM-OGRAM

Shortly after my 50th birthday, I received a letter in the mail from Cancer Care Ontario presenting me with the opportunity for another novel experience: my first mammogram. If you read my previous blog on my anxiety with people entering my peri personal space (see Mind Over Makeover), you would understand that this feat was not at the top of my "love to do" list. However, after reading the brochure which accompanied my letter, I realized that it needed to be on my "must do" list.

While I have had close family members who have died from cancer, including my Mom, breast cancer was not the cause. It was not until I read the brochure that accompanied the letter that I was stunned to learn that not only is more than 80% of breast cancer found in women over the age of 50, most of the women diagnosed have NO family history of the of the disease. Nonetheless, it took me over two months of reshuffling the letter from the kitchen counter, to the dining room table, and back to the kitchen before I picked up the phone to book an appointment; I think it was a combination of avoidance and our tendency to relegating self-care to the back burner at play.

I had heard horror stories from other women about the procedure – painful machinations involving the squishing of the ta-tas into torturous equipment by Nurse Rached look-alikes. On the morning of the appointment, I admit I was a little nervous. As it turned out, the procedure was both swift and, while somewhat uncomfortable, surprisingly painless. The technician explained the process in advance: four x-rays would be taken (two per breast, horizontal and vertical) using a machine with a plastic plate that pressed the breast in place for a few seconds while the x-ray was taken. The whole procedure would take less than 10 minutes. My technician was gentle and skilled and, fortunately, my proximal anxiety was minimal that day so, while I felt a little like Wham, Bam, Thank You Ma'am, it was more Dean Martin and less Urban Dictionary.

For all my half century girlfriends, I highly recommend that you take up the mantle of this feat. It is estimated that every year, 9,000 women in Ontario are diagnosed with breast cancer; unfortunately, almost 2,000 will still die from it. The upside is that breast cancer mortality continues to decline, likely due to both screening and better treatments. I can tell you that while the "Wham, Bam" wasn't the most enjoyable feat, I wholeheartedly support the "Thank You Mamm-ogram" part of the mantra.

October 5, 2015

PILLAR OF POSITIVITY #9:
Taking Care Of Your Mind—Mindfulness

I know that mindfulness is a word and concept that has saturated the popular media in the last few years. There are apps, books, and courses all designed to provide the latest Zen solution to our lives of stress, worry, and the general busy-ness that is pervasive in our modern world.

I admit that for a long time I equated mindfulness with an image of a monk sitting cross legged on a pillow, eyes closed and mind free of all thought. I was sure of two things: my fast-paced life was not in sync with spending time this way, and, even if I found the time, with my anxiety, there was no way I could ever "empty my mind." I concluded that mindfulness practices were simply not for me.

It was only when I began doing a little research into mindfulness that I started to change my understanding of what it really meant. According to Jon Kabat-Zin, mindfulness is "paying attention in a particular way, on purpose, in the present moment, and non-judgmentally." Nowhere in this definition was there a requirement to strike the lotus pose. Similarly, the need to empty one's mind of all its content was not necessary. I delved a bit deeper and discovered a host of benefits that had been determined through solid research practices: mindfulness had been found to slow down automatic responses; reduce stress; provide for a stronger immune system; and improve mental health. I decided that mindfulness required a second look.

Despite its recent popularity, mindfulness is far from a new concept; it has been a part of Eastern philosophy for thousands of years. However, with the growth of the field of positive psychology, mindfulness has been introduced as a scientific practice supporting improved health and wellbeing. It has also been developed as part of mental health treatments such as Mindfulness-Based Stress Reduction.

With a better understanding of mindfulness, I realized that there was no one "right" way to practice. I was not required to sit silently nor to have an empty mind; the idea wasn't to clear my mind, but to be aware of my thoughts, acknowledge them, and then, simply let them go. There was no pass/fail criteria and I was able to determine my own method. For me, mindfulness was – and is – about slowing down.

It wasn't an easy process and it did take me some time to let myself simply "be" with all that my "monkey mind" threw at me. I found that I preferred to practice my mindfulness "on the go;" that is, I learned to incorporate my mindful practice into my daily activities. Sometimes it was when I was out walking when I would become aware of the birds singing, the perfume of the lilac bushes, the feel of the wind through my hair. Occasionally I would stop and just appreciate the beauty of the moment. Other times I would recognize the stress of the moment, identify the emotion, and engage in a quiet few minutes of breathing, a grounding exercise, or a guided loving kindness meditation to bring me back to balance.

I am grateful to have discovered mindfulness in my life. It is a practice that I recommend to everyone moving through this wildly exciting, stressful, and beautiful world. For those who need a little support getting started, there are many resources available (many that are free) that will guide you through an assortment of activities until you find the one that works for you.

"Mindfulness isn't difficult. We just need to remember to do it." – Sharon Salzberg

August 8, 2017

#FABEAT: FEELING THE BEAT WITHOUT THE HEAT

While I don't play an instrument, am a little rhythm-challenged, and, as my kids can attest, cannot carry a tune in a bucket, music has always had a very special place in my heart. Good music just seems to connect directly to my soul and attending live concerts has come to be one of my favourite activities.

There is, however, a decided difference between being an enthusiastic audience member and participating in the creation of the music – I can feel the beat, but not necessarily keep the beat! Nonetheless, when I saw the flyer for a drumming circle event, I decided to stretch myself a little beyond my normal comfort zone by adding it as my next fabulous feat.

The drumming circle was being sponsored by the Canadian Mental Health Association – Niagara Branch and when I arrived at the location, I discovered that many participants were service users of CMHA, and their workers. Two Brock University students, who had heard about the event and came to check it out, rounded out the group of about 20 people.

The chairs were arranged in a circle, with a variety of exotic-looking drums, tambourines, maracas, and wooden instruments displayed in the centre. I sat at a chair between two gentlemen who were talking to another man at the head of the circle (if there is such a thing) about musical instruments, adaptors, and other details that escaped my limited understanding. I confess I started to get a little nervous about my non-musicianship status among some clearly experienced participants. A feeling washed over me that took me back to my grade 7 music class where cringe worthy noises escaped my recorder, no way resembling "Mary Had a Little Lamb".

I looked around the room as the other participants took their seats and was somewhat relieved to see similar expressions of discomfort on some other faces; a couple of individuals were turned slightly away from the circle, suggesting the possibility of fleeing was not out of the question. I felt a kinship with them.

Once everyone was settled, the man at the front of the circle addressed us: he said his name was Mark (Chino) and he had been drumming for over 15 years and working as a drum therapist-educator since 2005. He explained that everyone could create music, and that the workshop was about the joy of connecting with others and expressing ourselves through non-verbal communications, sharing a sacred space of trust, love and truth. His voice was gentle, and his smiling face invited us to let go of our fear and embrace the experience.

After his explanation, Mark invited us to select an instrument, but also acknowledged the legitimacy of choosing the role of listener. Most participants picked an instrument from the middle; I selected a maraca with, I admit, a bit of trepidation. A couple of people decided to sit quietly and observe the process – without judgment.

Over the next hour we learned a few rhythms, practiced together in unison, then in succession around the circle, first with eyes open, and then with eyes closed, using our sense of hearing to know when to take our turn. Mark lead us, encouraged us, celebrated us, throughout. I observed the comfort within the group grow as we started to work together. One man, who had initially been an observer, decided to tap his knee as we moved around the circle. When someone suggested that we change up our instruments by passing them to the person on our left, I was happy to accept the wooden block and even more pleased to see that those who had not chosen to use instruments actively accepted those that were given to them.

At the break we had a chance to talk about the experience so far. I talked to one participant about feeling "in tune" with the group and he told me about an experiment where pendulum clocks will, over time, synchronize in an "odd kind of sympathy" to each other because of the sound pulses. It was a nice analogy for me: while we all were from different situations and perspectives, through music, we came together. The music we created was the concrete representation of the connection we had made.

In fact, the use of music for joining groups together for healing dates back to ancient civilizations. Today, studies of music therapy have suggested that it can be used to enhance treatment for such health issues as depression by improving individuals' moods and allowing people to engage with each other in ways that words cannot convey (http://www. medicalnewstoday.com/articles/232150.php).

In the second half of the workshop, Mark accentuated our collaborative musical compositions with drums, bamboo flute, and the haunting sound of the didgeridoo. With each new song we created, our comfort with each other increased; the smiles multiplied, formerly hesitant participants leaned into the group. I surprised even myself when I noticed that once I became lost in the music, I was also able to keep the beat.

As we concluded our session, the man to my left told me he was inspired to start playing music again; the gentleman to my right was still humming a tune as I said goodbye. I walked to my car with not just another fabulous feat under my belt, but with a sense of calm, a smile on my face and a skip in my step.

October 31, 2015

#FABFEAT: MINDFUL MEDITATION AT SOUTH COAST GUEST HOUSE

One of the delightful things I have discovered as I work my way through my 50 feats is the incredible experiences that are available to me in my own backyard. Niagara is such an amazing place to live, but we sometimes become so accustomed to it that we don't look up and around as we make our mad dash through life.

This week, my slower pace of life was rewarded with a beautiful venue, lovely company, and a mindfulness experience that reminded me how to stay focused on the now, especially at this time of year.

I was fortunate enough to be one of the inaugural participants in the wellness programming being offered through a new venue in Port Colborne: The South Coast Guest House includes a beautiful house, incredibly peaceful wooded grounds within walking distance to the beach, and a brand-new guest house that is now accepting reservations for overnight guests. We were there for an afternoon of mindful meditation led by Maggie Denison, a gentle petite woman who has practiced meditation for decades and whose calm demeanor spoke to her practice.

Once everyone arrived, the dozen or so of us sat in chairs arranged in a circle. The room was surrounded by big windows that overlooked the tranquil grounds of the property; I could have simply rested peacefully watching the birds and felt I had more than my share of mindfulness.

Maggie's session provided us with two hours of guided meditation. With soft music and her soothing quiet voice, Maggie introduced us to the peace of deep breathing, the ease of a walking meditation practice, and the wonder of fully experiencing the sight, smell, and feel of a simple flower.

The beauty of this workshop was my ability to take away very practical steps that I can easily incorporate into my day without being overwhelmed by feeling I need to have a complicated meditation practice. Just three simple breaths upon awakening can set the tone for the day. A mindful walk around the kitchen can return calm at the end of a stressful day. The best part is there is no equipment needed- just your mind and body and a moment or two throughout the day.

The other benefit of the workshop was the ability to meet a group of new, like-minded women. During the break, I had a chance to chat with several of them and discovered one woman worked for CMHA-Niagara, and another was the daughter of a former colleague at Brock. We all expressed our interest in getting together again for another session, so comfortable were we with each other by the end of the experience.

This was the first of many wellness programs that are being introduced by The South Coast Guest House. I really look forward to attending more events in the future and maybe even treat myself and friends to an overnight stay at the guest house. If you want to learn more, or register for upcoming events, further details can be found on their Facebook page: Niagara's South Coast Guest House.

December 15, 2015

#FABFEAT: KICKIN' BACK IN KAUAI

When I had the opportunity to go to Kauai, I began to think about all the potential feats I could accomplish there: a helicopter ride, learning to surf, hiking down canyons, and ziplining over treetops.

The first morning, as I sat on the patio poring over the brochures of various activities, I noticed one of the Hawaiian geese, nene (pronounced nay-nay), walking towards me. The signs on the lawn warned that the nene were nesting nearby and the male birds were extremely protective of their territory, so I was a little nervous. But, the bird just came up on the patio stone and settled in next to me. I thought it was likely that other visitors had fed him before, so was sure that he would get bored and move away when there was no food coming his way. I was wrong. Each time I came out on the patio, Ralph, as I had named him, not only came over to sit with me, but RAN over as soon as the door opened. I don't know if birds smile, but if they do, Ralph was. One afternoon he brought another nene with him. In hindsight, I think it was his mother and it is possible that in bird-terms we are now married.

As we made our way to the various points of interest on the island, I found pleasure not only in the beautiful sights, but also in the unexpected encounters. At the Wailua Falls (they used these for the opening shot on Fantasy Island for those old enough to remember that show), I laughed as the man selling jewelry in the parking lot chatted with his friend, Oscar, a wild boar, standing just a few feet away. I swore I saw Oscar wag his tail upon hearing his name (this, I later found out, was true; pigs actually do wag their tails like dogs when they are happy). Once again, it is possible that food might have been involved in this friendship.

As the vacation unfolded, I felt less and less inclined to shoehorn a whole host of activities into each day. I decided that this feat would not be about a particular adventure, but a reminder to slow down and see the wonder in the every day. Okay, I recognize that a beautiful Hawaiian island is not ordinary, but that simply reinforced my point. I felt the Universe once again trying to make sure I got the message by sending me a sign – literally. And so, I did as a fish-shaped sign at the side of the road advised: Try Slow. I enjoyed morning walks listening to music, occasionally singing and dancing as the mood hit me, taking in the glory of the sand and the water; I sat in the sunshine and admired the trees blowing in the breeze; I marveled at the million-dollar view from the balcony of the St. Regis hotel at sunset that was free to anyone who came to have a look. I reflected on how incredibly fortunate I was not just to have been given the opportunity of this trip, but for all the many blessings in my life. As 2016 fast approaches, I look forward to the chapters ahead for me, big and small. I end 2015 with a better understanding of myself, and my priorities. Wishing everyone a very happy, healthy, and prosperous (however you define it) New Year!

January 2, 2016

PILLAR OF POSITIVITY #10:
Taking Care Of Your Soul - Spirituality

It has become increasingly common for people to distance themselves from religion and instead profess to being "spiritual." While I believe that everyone should be respected for their personal beliefs and I am in no way anti-religion, I must sheepishly admit that I am one of those people. My slight embarrassment is not about *being* spiritual, but that the term itself seems to have devolved into more of a fashion statement than a way of life.

I have always believed in what I described as the connectedness of all things. I think that my identification with the term spirituality began when I read Brené Brown's *The Gifts of Imperfection.* In Dr. Brown's words, "Spirituality is recognizing and celebrating that we are all inextricably connected to each other by a power greater than all of us, and that our connection to that power and to one another is grounded in love and compassion. Practicing spirituality brings a sense of perspective, meaning and purpose to our lives." In addition to the description of connectedness, the inclusion of love and compassion as anchors in these relationships spoke to my heart.

As I read more positive psychology research, this concept was further solidified by Sonja Lyubomirsky, who described spirituality as the "search for meaning in life through something that is larger than the individual self." Serving a greater meaning and purpose has been an important factor for me as I have developed my personal life perspective. This world view has fueled my passion for mental health awareness, community support and volunteerism, relationship building, and meditation practice.

Research supports not only the positive outcomes for a community when people participate in a spiritual way, but also for the practitioner directly. Benefits include increased lifespan, higher levels of reported happiness, improved relationships, and better mental and physical health. Spirituality provides for a win-win situation.

An unexpected outcome of exploring my own spirituality during my 50 Feats project was a newfound awareness of peace and awe that these activities provided. I *feel* connected to the world around me in a way that I previously didn't recognize. I now seek out opportunities to fulfil what I have defined as my purpose, and find meaning in the life I have chosen. My ability to use SilverLiningFrog.com to spread my thoughts and activities and, hopefully, inspire others to determine their own meaning and purpose, has blossomed as I developed my own understanding of what spirituality means for me.

I feel fortunate to have found my spiritual niche and extremely lucky to be able to live a life infused with meaning and purpose, connected to the world around me, and surrounded by people I love; that is my wish for everyone in a world that can be challenging and even heartbreaking at times.

"We are not human beings having a spiritual experience. We are spiritual beings having a human experience." – Pierre Teilhard de Chardin

September 5, 2017

#FABFEAT: MY SPIRITUAL BACKYARD

When I was creating my list of 50 Feats, I chose not to make a "bucket list," but rather to select novel activities that would impact my physical, mental, and spiritual wellbeing. On the spiritual side, I wondered about attending some kind of retreat. While I am not religious, I wanted to nurture my spiritual self, but I wasn't sure what that might look like. A quick internet search brought me to the Mount Carmel Spiritual Centre (http://www.carmelniagara.com/).

Located on Stanley Avenue in Niagara Falls, I have driven passed the Centre dozens of times over the years without knowing much about it other than to occasionally note how beautiful the buildings and grounds were. I thought it was a church, but never considered that it might be open to the public. The Monastery of Mount Carmel was constructed in 1894 as a hospice and spiritual retreat. Over the years it has served as a seminary and convent, and returned to its original purpose in 1979; today it hosts a variety of seminars and retreats on 10 beautiful acres of gardens, vineyards, and woods.

Serendipity was at play as I reviewed a list of the courses: Awakening to Happiness, Love, and Wisdom, a day-long workshop was being offered July 25. The description indicated that participants would learn the steps required to use our level of awareness to promote wholeness and wellbeing

– just up my alley. I called to reserve my spot and awaited the date.

The conference started at 9:30, but my companion, anxiety, has always ensured I am early to everything, so I had a good hour before the workshop. The upside of my "just in case" early arrival was having plenty of time to wander the grounds under a sunny, clear-blue sky, admiring the vivid green of the grape vines, and the majesty of the towering old brick structures. Other morning meanderers exchanged quiet hellos and shared a soft awe for our surroundings. I walked through the chapel and felt enveloped in its cool serenity. A quick peek into the offices gave me a glimpse of ancient book-laden shelves that harkened back to the roots of the monastery. Had my day ended here, I would have felt well served in the promotion of my wholeness and wellbeing.

The workshop consisted of 8 participants (all women) and the presenter. Half had been to Dr. Fazzari's workshops previously; the others, like me, were new to the experience. The time passed quickly as he shared information about recent neuroscientific research about the brain's ability to replace negative neural pathways with positive experiences and connections. The afternoon focused on love defined as a behaviour not a feeling – love as a verb rather than a noun. Finally, we considered the concept of success from a holistic, spiritual perspective: being happy with who you are, where you are, with what you have, and with whom you decide to share it.

After the workshop I reflected on the presentation of cutting-edge research in this century-old environment. The research was new, but the ideas aren't: joy, faith, hope, and love.

So how was my second fabulous feat? A little slower paced than the first, but exhilarating in its own way. My desire for meaning and purpose connected me with a group of strangers on their own spiritual journeys, and our hearts knew each other. How special and simple to learn that, if you only look, you can find these connections in your own spiritual backyard.

July 26, 2015

#FABFEAT: WHAT'S IN THE CARDS FOR ME?

I have never been to a psychic or had my palm, tea leaves, or cards read, but I have always been curious about the experience. My intrigue was fueled by watching episodes of The Amazing Kreskin as a child, and my Mom's uncanny ability to guess the "secret square" on Hollywood Squares more often than could be explained by chance.

When I mentioned my interest to my sons, the younger, Mr. Science, rolled his eyes and pointed to the million-dollar reward offered for anyone who could prove paranormal, supernatural, or occult powers that had remained unclaimed for more than 20 years. My older son, while skeptical, was willing to accompany me on my psychic adventure, albeit only when lured with the promise of lunch following the reading. I didn't know any psychics, so I again used the internet to find a local seer. My search brought me to Jewelee (askjewelee.com) who has been a psychic medium for over 25 years, and owns a new age shop in Niagara Falls from which she does readings, when not on the road at conventions and expos.

I originally intended my psychic adventure to take place a week earlier, but discovered Jewelee was in demand, requiring me to book more than a week in advance. The anticipation made the feat all the more fun. Jewelee's shop is in a little house on Victoria Avenue in Niagara Falls. We met her at the door and I liked her immediately – she had a welcoming smile and a down-to-earth style. As we got ready for the reading, she returned to the counter to give her rescue parrot some sunflower seeds to keep him occupied, noting that he was prone to swearing when feeling anxious. I felt an immediate kinship to this bird.

We decided to explore relationships, work, health, and finances in the session. While I won't reveal all of the specifics of her reading, I can say that she suggested I would find engaging employment in the next 6 months, that I would not move for at least the next 9 months, and I would not have financial or health problems for the foreseeable future.

She also did a quick read for my son. She talked about his career aspirations, suggesting that he was on the right track, but approaching it from the wrong angle. They discussed his ideas (he is creating table top games) and that he is trying to "leap to the top" when his success will come from keeping it small and introducing it locally. He appreciated the direction, whether psychically channeled or not.

Jewelee also read cards for my younger son, observing that he had high expectations for himself, and warning me to watch that he wasn't too hard on himself if he didn't reach his ideal. Ha, Mr. Science, she read you well!

In the end, I don't know if Jewelee had psychic abilities, but, regardless, I enjoyed the experience. And my son walked away feeling a sense of renewal for his game design work that no amount of advice from his mother could have provided. As for me, a little positive reinforcement as I look for full-time employment for the first time in 27 years, whatever its source, is more than welcome. All in all, I would say it was a feat well accomplished.

October 13, 2015

#FABFEAT: FULL MOON GHOST WALK

It has been a little bit more than a week between my feats recently. Having achieved one month at my new job, I am now starting to come up for air. I feel strongly that I am in the right place, but admit there is a lot for me to learn. Since my feats are meant to be a "positive psychology experiment," I am not getting stressed about being slightly behind; rather, I see that I am extending my enjoyment over a longer period – my story, and I'm sticking to it.

However, coming into the long weekend, I had a plan for this week's feat: St. Catharines' downtown association Full Moon Ghost Walk was on the calendar. Initially, I had suggested this activity as a "feat with friends," but forgot that it fell on a long weekend when people tend to head out of town to take advantage of the extra day and the first of the summer weather. While I am comfortable attending events solo, I decided to extend an invitation to The Navigator (previously introduced in the Isle of Wight adventure last summer) to join me. When I told my son of my plans, he articulated my own apprehension: "he'll definitely hate it." Knowing that the Navigator is a very logical creature, I decided to keep the nature of the evening's activity as a surprise; to his credit, he accepted my limited information of time (9 p.m.) and location (Market Square).

We arrived to find about a dozen other people milling about by the front of the square. The surprise was somewhat given away by the long black cape clad, lantern-toting tour guide, and I gleefully announced to the Navigator that we were going on a ghost walk. While I expected I might receive a little reluctance about participating, he shocked me by noting, with a smile, that there were similar walks in Ottawa. I exhaled a tiny sigh of relief – potential obstacle avoided.

The cape and lantern were juxtaposed against the IPad that our guide used to provide her own path and knowledge. We began by the old courthouse. As she stood on the steps and gave us some of the history, the clock on the tower chimed. Startled, our guide told us that in all the times she had given the tour, the clock had never chimed. By the side doors, she told us of the cramped cells that kept prisoners in the basement, where the stress of such close quarters occasionally caused one inmate to murder another. She also told us of the old slaughterhouse in the basement and the numerous reports of people hearing animal noises (or is it the cries of the ghostly prisoners?) in the space so many years later. When we moved on to the fountain out front, it, too, was surprisingly spouting water – another first for our guide. While the overcast sky didn't allow the moon to shine down on us, I felt some of the lunar effects were in play.

We moved about the downtown, stopping at churches, row houses, and parking lots. Each place was illustrated by its own story: an accidental death from a fall, a decapitation and subsequent hanging of the axe-wielding culprit, ghostly voices warning against an unseen danger, a gargoyle atop a building with an uncanny resemblance to an unpopular government official of the time. The tour ended at Merritt House. I had no knowledge of the long history of paranormal activity associated with the present site of several radio stations. As our guide stood on "Oak Hill," she described the numerous recorded events, including hearing voices, seeing ghostly reflections in windows, and bizarre closing of doors and movements of articles. She referred to an on-air moment when an other-worldly voice broke into a broadcast with an proclamation that those in earshot "go to hell." (I looked that one up after the walk and listened to the recording. It was eerie).

Throughout the hour and a half, I kept an eye on The Navigator to determine his reaction to the tour. Each time the guide provided information about the various events, activities, and historical contexts, he seemed engaged, smiling and laughing along with the rest of the participants. I was impressed, but remembered that, in addition to being a skeptic, he was also a historian. As we walked back to the car after the tour, he expressed his enjoyment of the evening. Going out on a limb, I asked "So, do you believe in ghosts now?" to which he smiled and simply replied "No." So, while I have a healthy interest in the possibilities of the extraordinary, apparently you don't have to believe to enjoy the ride.

May 28, 2016

#50 FABULOUS FEATS: THE MOVEMENT

Here it is: the last of my 50 Fabulous Feats! When I began this journey on my 50th birthday, I couldn't have imagined the incredible people, places, and things I would encounter along the way. I began the blog as an applied positive psychology experiment and, while it involved less than sound research methodology, I feel quite confident that I am the better for having engaged in this array of awesome activities. As I complete my 50 Feats, I have been reflecting on the learning because of practicing these pillars of positivity:

Practicing Gratitude: According to Robert Emmons, gratitude is "a felt sense of wonder, thankfulness, and appreciation for life." For me, it involved giving back to my community, particularly in recognition of the privilege I enjoy. My passion in mental health was reflected in my contributions to the Women and Wellness fundraiser through Canadian Mental Health Association – Niagara Branch. My wish to support those living without the basic life necessities that we take for granted, including food and shelter, led me to volunteer with the great people at Start Me Up Niagara and the Coldest Night of the Year walk as well as the Niagara Region when it conducted its first point-in-time survey of homelessness. The wonderful 100 Women Who Care – Niagara further showed me both the needs within my community and the positive difference a small group of people can have when they come together for a common cause. Research more reliable than my own experiment has identified the benefits of practicing gratitude to be higher self-esteem, energy, and hopefulness; increased ability to cope with stress; decreased envy, loneliness, and anxiety; and a building of social bonds. I know that as I look back, these outcomes resonate with me.

Cultivating Optimism: Sonja Lyubormirsky describes optimism as "finding the silver lining in a cloud. Not only celebrating the present and past, but anticipating a bright future." I feel a kindred spiritedness with Dr. Lyubormirsky as many of my feats focus on the silver lining and hope associated with the ability to live well with mental illness. I had the opportunity to share my story of ongoing recovery from the perspective of someone both living with mental illness and as the mother of a young adult son who also has mental health challenges. Rather than focusing on the struggles, and there are many of them, we have chosen to create our own silver linings. One of my favourite feats continues to be when Christian and I got matching semi-colon tattoos symbolizing the importance of recognizing mental illness as a pause in the story and not the end. Equally as memorable was my opportunity to meet Dr. Barbara Fredrickson (I call her my "rock star researcher") whose Broaden and Build Theory was foundational to my 50 Feats; she posits that positive emotions like joy, contentment, and love help people to be open to new ideas (broaden) that, in turn, allows individuals to grow their physical, intellectual, and social resources (build) which can later be drawn upon for coping and resilience in the face of challenges. In addition, cultivating optimism has been found to support the achievement of goals, positive mood, and high energy. I feel strongly that my own positive focus has been the driving force for my psychological growth and ability to bounce back – Thanks Barbara!

Practicing Acts of Kindness: We all can practice acts of kindness – selfless acts in support of others. Interestingly, such activities have been found to produce greater benefits for the giver than the receiver – truly a win-win proposition. From blood donation (while I wasn't able to do so for health reasons, others told me that my blog inspired them to donate in my stead), to building a playground with likeminded strangers, to planting trees to reduce my carbon footprint, I accomplished these fabulous feats spending zero dollars in the process showing that such acts are accessible and possible for everyone. Reviewing the benefits of elevated happiness, increased compassion, social connection, confidence, and optimism, I wholeheartedly believe I was the benefactor in every case.

Nurturing Social Relationships: Researcher/storyteller Brene Brown writes: "we are biologically, cognitively, physically, and spiritually wired to love, to be loved, and to belong." This statement struck a chord for me not just because I have always been relationship-driven in my life, but also because those of us who live with mental illness share a common dichotomous challenge: when we are unwell, we tend to socially isolate at a time when we need to connect more than ever. Many of my feats revolved around activities with others – friends and strangers alike. Whether eating snails, horseback riding, learning to cook, or touring local sights and sounds of Niagara, the experience was enhanced because I was sharing it with others. According to research, those who cultivate connections have the benefit of strengthened immune systems, longer life, lower levels of anxiety and depression, and greater empathy. Excitingly, the positive results of nurturing social relationships are bi-directional which means that not only was I made happier by my connections, but, as a more positive person, I also enjoy a greater likelihood of acquiring new friends.

Developing Coping Strategies: Sonja Lyubormirsky describes coping strategies as "what people do to alleviate the hurt, the stress or suffering caused by a negative event or situation." Engaging in problem-focused and emotion-focused techniques and practices allow me to not just survive, but thrive while living with mental illness, supporting post-traumatic growth and transformation. In some instances, my "feats" were very specific to me: the makeover that invaded my peri-personal space; travelling alone to Ottawa; and successfully navigating the mental health system of "hospital-land" with my son. In each case, I emerged with a sense of meaning and purpose, one of the benefits supported by the research into coping strategies.

Savouring Life's Joys: According to Dr. Fredrickson, savouring involves "considering good events in such a way that you willfully generate, intensify, and prolong your heartfelt enjoyment of them." Savouring allows you to triple the pleasure through anticipation, experiencing, and remembering events. As I write this, I am smiling as I think about my first feat of riding a motorcycle, re-experiencing that enjoyment after all these months. My nose piercing still glints at me every morning when I look in the mirror and, if I close my eyes, I can feel the whoosh and hear the roar of the wind as I ziplined down the Niagara gorge. Savouring is the gift that keeps on giving.

Committing to Your Goals: Moving towards individual intentions, wishes, and desires has been shown to increase self-esteem, confidence, and provide meaning and purpose, especially when the goals are intrinsic and authentic to you. It is important to note that the benefits arise from approaching something you want rather than from moving away from something undesirable. I get a little emotional when reviewing this pillar. Neale Walsch said "life begins at the edge of your comfort zone;" 50 Fabulous Feats empowered me to push my limits and achieve beyond my wildest imagination. I obtained my Master of Education degree, started my own consulting business, became a certified Coach Practitioner, landed my dream job of Recovery Support Worker, and completed training as a SPARKie with the Mental Health Commission of Canada. Sharing these accomplishments through my blog further served to enhance the thrill of each achievement.

Taking Care of Your Body, Mind, and Soul: The World Health Organization defines health as "a state of complete physical, mental, and social well-being and not merely the absence of disease or infirmity." The importance of taking care of yourself is not a new concept, especially related to the benefits of physical activity. In fact, some research has found that physical exercise can have as much, and sometimes more, of an effect in improving mental health issues, such as depression, as medication. My fab feats included not just walking around the neighbourhood (listening to the audio recording of Moby Dick), but also around the Isle of Wight (104 km in 6 days). From a mental health perspective, I pursued mindful activities including drumming, meditation, and, my favourite, kickin' back in Kauai, in support of reduced stress, stronger immunity, and just plain slowing down in a world that sometimes feels like it moves at warp speed. Finally, I explored what Sonja Lyubomirsky describes as the "search for meaning in life through something that is larger than the individual self." In my case, it was not connected to organized religion (although I wholly support others who choose this path), but through considering various aspects of spirituality including a retreat at a spiritual centre on the one hand, and a psychic reader on the other. Of note is the prediction from Jewelee that my next position would involve "travelling from one place to another" rather than working at a single location; my time is now spent visiting clients in the community to support their health and wellbeing as an Assertive Community Treatment Team (ACTT) member which infuses my soul with meaning and purpose every day.

And so, I conclude my applied positive psychology experiment in this, my 50th blog. After spending over a year engaging in novel, engaging activities in support of increasing my own positive affect, however, I believe that the impact of these pillars of applied positive psychology is too important to simply end. I think everyone can benefit from a little "broaden and build" activity. And so, I am rolling out the next phase of my applied positive psychology experience: Fabulous Feats: The Movement.

This "final" blog launches a call to action for others to take up the mantle, engaging in your own unique, novel, interesting feats, and sharing them with the world. I will be assisting the movement through introducing one of the positive psychology pillars and inviting your posts, pictures, tweets, and videos illustrating how you have embraced the ideas through your own activities. As I complete this post, I am simultaneously unveiling my own Facebook page: **Fabulous Feats**, that I would love for you to "like" and, where we can, share our ongoing experiences.

In addition, I would love for you to support the movement through the hashtag campaign: **#FabFeats** with a quick tweet about your own activities. SilverLiningFrog.com will continue with posts describing research and suggestions that you might try based upon each month's positivity pillar.

For December, the focus will be on **Practicing Gratitude**. In keeping with the theme, I would like to thank everyone who has supported SilverLiningFrog and my Fabulous Feats throughout the journey so far. I appreciate you more than words can say.

November 28, 2016

CONCLUSION: FABFEATS - THE JOURNEY CONTINUES...

As I approached my 50th birthday, I decided to embark on an adventure to engage in interesting activities that were new to me and blog about them. The research suggested that I could positively impact my own mood through such an exercise and I wanted to put it to the test. Little did I know that 50 Fabulous Feats @ 50 would change my life so profoundly. As I look back, I am incredibly thankful for the opportunities, my ability to share them with my community, and the learning that I experienced from each and every fabulous feat, big and small.

Some people have asked me what my favourite feat has been. It is difficult to choose – they are all special in their own way. I do treasure the matching semi-colon tattoo my older son and I got together; we are united in the hope for tomorrow for those facing mental health challenges. I am proudest of walking the coastal path of the Isle of Wight – 104 km in 6 days! My performance wasn't pretty, but I did it and, despite being woefully unprepared physically for this adventure, I enjoyed the breathtaking views, the kindness of strangers, the unexpected moments - like passing a field of grazing llamas.

When I talk about my favourite feats, however, I always add the qualification "so far." You see, the journey continues. When I presented my project at the Mental Health Commission of Canada's Supporting the Promotion of Activated Research and Knowledge (SPARK) training, the first thing my mentor said to me was "you need to add a '+' onto 50; this project shouldn't have an end." He was right. It is a lifestyle now as each day I look for new opportunities to tap into the 10 Pillars of Wellness: Practicing Gratitude, Cultivating Optimism, Practicing Acts Of Kindness, Nurturing Social Relationships, Developing Coping Strategies, Savouring Life's Joys, Committing To Your Goals, Taking Care Of Your Body (Physical), Mind (Mindfulness), and Spirit (Spirituality). Sometimes, it is as simple as taking a new trail with my doggie friends when we go for our daily constitutional. Other times it is a big step into the unknown, like recently launching the website for **Susan Mifsud Consulting Services** or starting my role as the inaugural LinkedIn Pulse Blogger for Healthy Minds Canada focused on workplace wellness **(Working On Wellness)**.

While the experiment itself doesn't end, the researcher in me desires an evaluation of whether engaging in interesting, novel activities had a positive impact on me. Although my assessment techniques are less than scientific, I can say that I experienced a boost in my energy levels, was motivated to complete goals, gained greater social connection, and experienced an ability to cope with stressful situations with fewer mental and physical health challenges. This past summer I was a juror on an 8+

week criminal trial that changed my routines and exposed me to traumatic circumstances. I ensured that I practiced my pillars including walking during lunch hours, recording those things for which I am grateful, engaging in random acts of kindness, connecting with friends and family, journaling as a coping strategy, and practicing mindful meditation. While no one can emerge unchanged by such an experience, I maintained my own wellness and, hopefully, contributed positively to the wellbeing of my fellow jurors. Though anecdotal in nature, I do believe my foray into positive psychology practices have changed me for the better.

In my 50 Feats posts, I ended each blog with "Up Next" which gave a preview of the upcoming adventure the following week. I am thrilled to say that it has become kind of a habit now, hardwiring me to look for those novel, intentional activities that bring joy, satisfaction, peace, kinship, and thankfulness. I continue to share the benefits of practicing positive psychology with others. I look forward to presenting "50 Feats" in a Power Talk at the **Niagara Leadership Summit for Women** with its theme of Breaking Barriers. I am also in the process of converting my blogs into a book highlighting the Pillars of Wellness and my adventures.

I want to thank everyone who has joined me on my blog travels, both in person and virtually. I hope that I have inspired you to engage in your own "Fabulous

Feats" and that you have experienced their positive outcomes. On this Thanksgiving weekend, I know that I am truly blessed, and I send thoughts of love and laughter to all my family and friends for a joyous weekend and fabulous adventures ahead.

Wishing you wellness, Susan

October 8, 2017

Join me on my continued journey:

Blog: **SilverLiningFrog.com**
Facebook: **Fabulous Feats**
Twitter: **@RoxyMae**
Website: **SusanMifsudConsulting.com**

References

Brown, B. (2010). *The gifts of imperfection: Let go of who you think you're supposed to be and embrace who you are.* Centre City, Minnesota: Hazelden Publishing.

Brene, B. (2012). *Daring greatly; How the courage to be vulnerable transforms the way we live, love, parent, and lead.* New York: Penguin Random House.

Brown, S. L. (2008, May). Play is more than just fun [Video file]. Retrieved from http://www.ted.com/talks/stuart_brown_says_play_is_more_than_fun_it_s_vital

Bryant, F. B., & Veroff, J. (2017). *Savoring: A New Model of Positive Experience.* New Jersey, NY: Lawrence Erlbaum Associate Inc. Publishers.

Emmons, R. A., and Shelton, C. M. (2002). Gratitude and the science of positive psychology. In Snyder, C. R., and Lopez, S. J. (eds.). *Handbook of Positive Psychology* (pp. 459-71). Oxford: Oxford University Press.

Fredrickson, B. (2009). *Positivity.* New York: Crown Publishers.

Kabat-Zinn, J., & University of Massachusetts Medical Center/Worcester. (1991). *Full catastrophe living: Using the wisdom of your body and mind to face stress, pain, and illness*. New York, NY: Pub. by Dell Pub., a division of Bantam Doubleday Dell Pub. Group.

Lyubomirsky, S. (2014). *The myths of happiness: What should make you happy but doesn't, what shouldn't make you happy but does*. New York: Penguin Books.

Lyubomirsky, S. (2008). *The how of happiness: A scientific approach to getting the life you want*. New York: Penguin Press.

Melville, H. (2017). *Moby Dick*. London: Alma Books.

Neff, K. (2015). *Self-Compassion: Stop beating yourself up and leave insecurity behind*. London: Yellow Kite.

Sambo, C. F., Forster, B., Willams, S. C., & Iannetti, G. D. (2012). To blink or not to blink: Fine cognitive tuning of the defensive peripersonal space. *The Journal of Neuroscience, 32(37):12921–12927; doi:10.1523/ JNEUROSCI.0607-12.2012*

Weiner, E. (2013). *The Geography of Bliss: One Grump's Search for the Happiest Places in the World*. New York: Time Warner Trade Publishing

www.ingramcontent.com/pod-product-compliance
Lightning Source LLC
Chambersburg PA
CBHW051042250726
48656CB00001B/99